Migraine-Free Cooking!

Heidi Gunderson

Migraine-Free Cooking! / Heidi Gunderson

ISBN: 978-0-557-21320-7

Acknowledgments

I would first like to thank Dr. David Buchholz for healing *my* headaches. Without his book, I would find myself in a whirlwind of headaches, pain, dizziness, and prescription medication. Healing my headaches has made my relationships with friends, and especially family, much more enjoyable. I would also like to thank Dr. Buchholz for allowing me to write a cookbook based on his findings. It is my goal to raise awareness about his method for healing headaches in order to help others, and I believe a cookbook is the best way I can contribute. I am happy to have the opportunity to help people.

I would like to thank my husband and best friend, Mike, for his support through my book-writing experience. I've cooked many recipes and spent a lot of time on the computer away from my family, and he has been extremely supportive and helpful. We have two small boys named Connor and Payton, and he has spent many nights alone with them to give me time to write. John and Mary, his mom and step-dad, have also been very helpful and supportive.

Thank you to my mom, Nancy, and my grandparents, Eldon and Charlene, for your guidance and support. And thank you to George and Dorothy, for you have been such a positive light.

Thank you to Rachel Gunderson, Brian McGee, Elizabeth Rulifson, and others for your wonderful editing skills. Without you this book would not say what it is supposed to say. Thank you also to Joseph C. Dix II for sharing your vast computer expertise so my website could be just the way I wanted it to be.

I would like to thank God for taking me on this miraculous journey. God has always rained his favor down on me, and I know this book is one big thunderstorm.

I would like to thank all of my doctors for seeing me through the pain and into the sunshine. I could not have done it without any of you. Thank you especially to Mark Buckingham and Jennifer Ravenscroft for your help and support.

Last but not least, I would like to thank all of my family and friends for encouraging me to write this cookbook in the first place. Pursuing this dream was much easier with the support network I had around me. There are many people who played a role in this experience whom I have not mentioned by name, but thank you to them as well.

Contents

Introduction

Like many, I have suffered from migraines since childhood. After numerous visits to the doctor and several failed attempts at finding a proper treatment plan, I was left frustrated and exhausted. When I thought there was nowhere else to turn, I was introduced to a method that changed my life. I had been told about migraine triggers before, but never in such a clear manner. Dr. Buchholz's 1-2-3 method was different than any other method I had tried before. There is no cure for migraines, but there are ways to eliminate the causes of painful blood vessel swelling in the head and other aspects of the migraine mechanism. The better I felt, the more people I told about the method. To my surprise, they didn't feel happy for me; they felt sorry for me. Why? I was on a diet that restricted me from eating foods that many people enjoy every day. I realized that those around me were as uneducated about migraine prevention as I once was. Most of those around me who also suffered from migraines turned to medication as their only hope of relief. Those individuals I encountered who were aware that migraines could be brought on by diet yearned for recipes that are trigger free, like the ones you'll find in this cookbook. There are even a few tips to help you cook some of your old favorites the migraine-friendly way. The recipes taste great and are easy to understand and prepare. This book was made for the everyday kitchen. If you're ready to take control of your headaches with mouth watering recipes and a method that actually works, this book is for you! I spent nearly two years researching nutrition and cooking methods to bring you the best possible recipes.

From Fight to Flight: My headache Story

It's amazing how much a person with migraines will suffer before realizing the need to seek help. Usually it's because symptoms build gradually enough that they elude the migraineur, and the problem can no longer be ignored. Therefore, help has to be sought due to overwhelming pain or tragedy. This was definitely true in my case. I tell my story so you know that I understand the agony, heartache, and fear you feel. There is nothing wrong with you, and you are not alone. Many people are in our shoes. My experiences led me to write this book. If you haven't already, I hope someday you will also turn lemons into lemonade.

Headaches plagued me even as a little girl. As a child, they were preceded by nosebleeds that had to be cauterized and packed in the emergency room. In young adolescence, they were coupled with back pain and also what I thought were sinus troubles. I remember the agony of the pounding pressure well, although it still had not yet reached its peak. In late adolescence, I had headaches almost every day, some preceded by flashing lights. This is why my doctor diagnosed them as migraines, even though many people, including members of my own family, believed them to be *all in my head*. What was the most hurtful, even to this day, was that people believed I was making this up. Perhaps you've had similar experiences. My doctor prescribed a medication in the triptan family called Imitrex. Triptans stop the migraine mechanism dead in its tracks, although they do not work on all migraine sufferers. Imitrex, one of the few triptans offered at the time of my diagnosis, didn't work on my headaches and made me feel as if my head would implode instead of explode. The next time I saw my doctor she took me off of the Imitrex and dismissed the possibility of migraines as the source of my symptoms. As a result, I continued to have headaches, a drippy, stuffy nose, and excruciating back pain, still - always.

While attending college, I tried many over-the-counter medications. I drank eight to nine cups of sugar-infused, caffeinated beverages a day, – anything to feel better. The pressures of life were time consuming, and I did not have time to deal with headaches. I just wanted to fix the problem quickly and get back to my life.

Pregnancy was hard with my first child. The only medications allowed were Tylenol and Sudafed. No caffeine! Needless to say, it was a rough ride. My obstetrician was the first person to ever introduce me to healthy eating. Let me say that again; my obstetrician was the first person to ever introduce me to healthy eating. She asked me if I was eating enough fiber and protein, and I didn't know how to answer her. She told me to reduce my sugar intake. I didn't realize that meant more than eliminating soda and donuts, nor did I know how to read nutrition labels. In today's world of fast food and prepackaged, boxed foods, people don't always realize what is in the food they eat. I read labels and cut out sugars and fats to the best of my ability, but I still gained weight and felt horrible due to the preservatives hidden in those foods. Also, I didn't eat enough fiber and carbohydrates in the form of fruits and vegetables, and I didn't know foods were triggering my headaches. You see, many reduced-fat or low-fat foods have extra migraine triggers added to them to enhance flavor. After my first son, Connor, came into the world, I didn't feel any better, but I didn't care because he was absolutely wonderful!

My second pregnancy was worse. I was an orchestra teacher, which is a wonderful, but stressful job. During the first trimester, I began to lose eyesight in one eye for seconds at a time. I would stand in front of my classroom to teach and have to pause until the episode passed to continue with my lesson. Luckily, they didn't last long, so the students barely noticed. I attributed my vision loss to the pregnancy. At times I felt faint and dizzy, symptoms which I also attributed to the pregnancy. One day, I was driving to work in bumper-to-bumper six-lane traffic, with cars speeding and slowing like jet skis near a crowded beach, when suddenly everything before me went black and I felt as if I were going to faint. My son Connor was in the backseat, and there is no doubt in my mind that if my "mommy instincts" had not kicked in, I would have fainted. I slowed down, white knuckled, with what I believed the flow of traffic to be until my eyesight came back, and after thanking God profusely for saving our lives, I drove to work. The funny thing is, I still didn't realize I had a problem. My principal and secretary called in a substitute and told me to visit the doctor. I thought they were crazy. I was fine! Weird things happen during pregnancy, right? Then they looked at me as if I were the crazy one and told me to call for a ride so that I didn't have to drive myself to the doctor. I agreed to contact someone, just to put them at ease, of course. About one half hour later, I began to feel a headache gradually creep in, and it soon became the worst migraine I had ever felt in my lifetime. My wonderful obstetrician took tests to make sure everything was normal and then sent me to see a neurologist as a wonderful obstetrician should.

This was the beginning of my journey with neurologists. The first one told me to drink three caffeinated beverages a day as a migraine preventive and did not address diet at all. He did, however, run a series of tests. His reasoning for the caffeine was that I couldn't take medication due to the fact that I was pregnant. I guess I could drink a drug harmful to fetuses, though? After my second son, Payton, was born, I saw a second neurologist who told me that "neurologists make most of their money from migraine patients and that is how they afford to live in their big fancy houses." He then proceeded to send me home with narcotic after narcotic and told me I did not need a preventive. I didn't want to mask the pain; I wanted to fix it! I liked my third neurologist; he at least addressed diet as an issue. He also started me on a preventive medication and experimented with triptans, of which more were available than in my teenage years, but they still didn't work for me. I was still dizzy and losing eyesight, nauseous, and depressed; I was miserable.

It was at this time that my mom visited the Mayo Clinic for Shogrin's disease and ran into a lovely lady who also suffered from migraines. A neurologist at the clinic told the lady to read *Heal Your Headache: the 1-2-3 Program for Taking Charge of Your Pain* by David Buchholz, M.D. The book changed my life, and I know it will change yours too. You are not alone. There are millions of us who experience severe symptoms and feel like we have nowhere to turn. I started the diet and felt a huge difference in two weeks. I also stopped taking all of the pain killers with which my third neurologist was experimenting. The combination lead me down a road I didn't know existed. I almost felt as if I could fly after so many years of fighting! The longer I followed the diet, the better I felt.

Two months later, I left my third neurologist to be in the care of one who gives a copy of *Heal Your Headache* to all of his migraine patients. I no longer experience headaches or any of the severe accompanying symptoms on a daily basis. I still occasionally have back pain due to barometric pressure changes in the atmosphere, but I'm hopeful that this too will subside in the near future. I take a very low-dose preventive, and I am not ashamed of it. I follow the diet to the best of my ability, but I do enjoy eating out or at friends' houses occasionally. My friends know I'm on a special diet, but bless their hearts, have no idea how to cook for it, even though they are sweet to try. In the past, without the preventive, one little slip and I had a headache. Now, as long as I follow the diet 90-95% of the time, I am still in control. I enjoy no longer living in a prison. I feel like a person now, not a victim.

Relearn How to Shop and Cook

Retailers make quick-prepare meals due to our fast-paced society. When my grandmother was young, they didn't exist; every meal was made from scratch. Many of the boxed, canned, or meal-in-a-bag foods in the supermarket are not hard to make on your own from scratch, but people have simply forgotten how. These foods are unhealthy, fatty, full of sugar and salt, and loaded with preservatives that I can't pronounce. Now people complain about how unhealthy these foods are, which means people are beginning to pay attention, but when fat, sugar and salt are taken out of prepared foods, flavorings have to be added to make them taste better and so do extra preservatives to keep them edible, if they can be called that. Sugar and salt are natural preservatives, so artificial ones have to be added when the others are taken away. As a migraineur, there are certain preservatives and flavorings your body does not process well: MSG, MSG-derivatives, nitrates, nitrites, sulfites, fermentation, and even the aging process of some foods which causes a build-up of tyramine (Buchholz 76, 83).

So, the moral of that story is to buy fresh, and when you can't, check labels. Check for nitrates or nitrites, sulfites, MSG, or any other triggers listed in Dr. Buchholz's book. Once I became used to labels and the types of foods I could eat, the most frustrating trigger to avoid was onions, which contain tyramine (87). There are many foods- foods which would make it easier to cook- that claim to be free of MSG, but even so, onions or onion powder would still be in the ingredients. I remember a trip to the health food store in desperation for chicken stock because I was tired of cooking whole chickens, and I was sure that I could find a brand that used shallots instead of onions there. Well, I found one that used shallots *and* onions. I wanted to hurl it across the store! What is the purpose of that? So, I was back to preparing whole chickens. The pure stock from whole chickens tastes better anyway. Friends, it's not that hard to put a whole chicken in the oven. It takes about two hours to cook, and I've found it's cheaper as well. The meat lasts for two to three meals, and I can usually gather about a cup and a half of stock or more from a chicken – no flavorings or preservatives added. I can get even more stock from turkey. If I boil everything leftover after the meat is taken off of the bones, adding some vegetables to the pot, I can get even more stock.

Chicken stock can be used to make cream of mushroom or cream of chicken soup, which livens up just about any meal. You can use it to make pan sauce or as a tenderizer. Beef stock can be obtained by making roast in a Dutch oven and spooning out the broth. It can also be used to make a soy sauce substitute or teriyaki sauce. All of these recipes are in this cookbook. Everything in this book is designed to help you learn to cook from scratch if you are an amateur cook or for ideas to flavor meals the trigger-free way if you are a novice cook. Feel free to experiment and change as needed to fit your specific needs and tastes. We are all individuals with different pallets and dietary needs. The most important thing is to *enjoy yourself*!

The Book Behind the Diet

Heal Your Headache: The 1-2-3 Program for Taking Charge of Your Pain is a wonderful book written by Dr. David Buchholz at The Johns Hopkins University School of Medicine. It explains in detail exactly which foods are headache triggers and tells how to avoid them. This cookbook is based on Dr. Buchholz's methods, and the diet mentioned in this book will not work without the rest of the program. If you think you know what foods are triggers and have trouble finding yours, you have not tried his method yet. It works! Patients who were once deemed "incurable" were able to find normalcy through the use of his methods. Dr. Buchholz also explains why there are so many myths about headaches and tells exactly what those myths are. If you are tired of being in pain, tired of being on medications and see no end in sight for you, this is the book to purchase. As Dr. Buchholz explains, you *do not* have to live with your headaches!

Exercise, Sleep and Positive Thinking

Changing your diet is a huge, positive step toward healing your headaches. However, there are other steps to take as well. One of those steps is to understand the power of positive thinking. Living in pain can weigh down on a spirit. Surround yourself with positive influences as much as possible, with happy friends and family, and remember to have fun. I understand that this can be hard when you are in pain. It may be helpful to find a support group of other headache sufferers. Don't let migraines ruin your relationships with friends and family. Your headache isn't important; you are. Negative thinking and dwelling on the headache may only make the pain worse. Your pain is real. Please believe that I am not discounting the pain you are feeling. However, it is important to believe that you are healing and that this pain will not last forever. Do you believe it is possible to get better? Positive thinking will help you heal.

It is also important to exercise daily. A little bit of cardiovascular exercise can really help a migraine sufferer. Don't forget to stretch and drink plenty of liquids. Stretching your neck and shoulder area is especially important. Migraines can cause the symptom of muscle tension in the neck and shoulders. Stretching this area daily may help relieve headaches. I personally have to stretch this area, along with my back and hamstrings, three times a day. I stretch every other major muscle in my body once a day. When the barometric pressure falls, I may need to do a little extra. Consult your doctor for an appropriate exercise regime.

Are you sleeping enough at night? Migraineurs require eight to nine hours of sleep every night on the same schedule (Buchholz 62). Life may get in the way every once in awhile, but don't let it happen often. Your head can't take it. If you have trouble sleeping, it may be beneficial to read a book on effective sleep habits before trying medication. Both lack of exercise and stress can get in the way of restful sleep. There may be other factors affecting your slumber as well.

Frequently Asked Questions

Question: Onions are a trigger. Is onion powder?
Answer: Yes.

Question: I was told tannins are a trigger. Is that true?
Answer: Tannins are found in the skin of red apples and in red wine. They are not a trigger on Dr. Buchholz's list. The culprits in red wine are fermentation and tyramine. Enjoy all the apples, red or otherwise, that you wish. It is best not to drink, but if you must, distilled vodka is your best option. Just think the clearer and less fermented, the better.

Question: Should I avoid tomatoes? I don't know whether they are a trigger or not.
Answer: Tomatoes can be a trigger for some due to the high amounts of free glutamate. This is not to be confused with wheat gluten. Mushrooms and peas pose the same problem. So, why not enjoy tomatoes unless you know for sure that they are a trigger? The diet can feel limiting as it is. Eliminate all other triggers, and if you still are not happy with the result, eliminate tomatoes, mushrooms and peas. If it makes no difference after two to four weeks, add them back in (Buchholz 88).

Question: Are there chicken or vegetable broths that follow the diet?
Answer: Many chicken and vegetable broths contain monosodium glutamate (MSG). There are some broths that do not. When buying at the store, the best option is to buy organic vegetable broth that contains no MSG, or chicken stock instead of chicken broth (MSG free). However, these broths are still prepared with onions, which means they contain tyramine. So, in the beginning stages of the diet, it is necessary to make your own chicken stock. After you have your headaches under control, you may find that you can substitute one of the others once in awhile.

Question: Are green onions safe?
Answer: Yes. Green onions are the same as scallions. The names are interchangeable. Spring onions, also safe, are a larger form of green onion with a larger bulb and more potent taste. Shallots are small bulbous white onions with brown skins. They are also safe. So is garlic. So, your onion choices are leeks, shallots, and green onions (also known as scallions or spring onions) (87).

Question: Is milk a trigger?

Answer: Milk is not a trigger. There are some milk products which contain tyramine that are triggers. Avoid cheese, yogurt, frozen yogurt, sour cream, and buttermilk. You may enjoy milk, cottage cheese, ricotta cheese, cream cheese, and high-quality American cheese from the deli, but be sure to check the ingredients as always (83-84).

Question: Are artificial sweeteners triggers?

Answer: Aspartame is a trigger. Saccharin (Sweet n' Low) may also be a trigger for some. Other artificial sweeteners, including sucralose (Splenda) are okay (87).

Question: Many of these recipes contain sugar and salt. Do they cause headaches?

Answer: Sugar and salt are not triggers. Too much sugar and salt may contribute to dehydration, which can trigger a headache. Eat it in moderation, and drink enough water. And remember, even though a recipe calls for a half teaspoon or teaspoon of salt, you only eat one helping of that recipe which contains much less. Enjoy a little bit of flavor in your food. If this still doesn't satisfy you, reduce the amount of salt in the recipes to fit your liking. Or, you may use natural sea salt which you don't need to add as much of for the same salty flavor. It can be found in health food stores if your grocery store doesn't carry it.

Question: Are decaffeinated teas and coffees safe?

Answer: Even decaffeinated teas and coffees contain natural chemicals that can start the migraine mechanism in some people. In the beginning, they are best avoided. Add them back in one at a time later on, like every other trigger, to see if they are a problem for you. Avoid any flavored teas or coffees that contain additional triggers, like lemon or orange teas or mocha coffees (76-77).

Shopping Lists
(Everything in the recipes)

Dairy (avoid non-fat dairy, but low-fat is okay without trigger preservatives)

All-natural ice cream

American cheese slices from deli

Cottage cheese

Cream cheese or Neufchatel cheese

12 oz. evaporated milk

Heavy whipping cream

Milk

Ricotta cheese

Fish

Canned crab, not preserved with hydrolyzed protein

Canned tuna, not preserved with hydrolyzed protein

Clams

Fillets – perch, sole, cod, haddock, or other lean fish fillets, about ¾ inch thick

Oysters

Steaks – salmon, trout, whitefish, catfish, carp, herring, tuna, or other medium-fat or fatty fish steaks

Shrimp – fresh or frozen with tails, deveined if possible

Fruits

Apples or applesauce

Blueberries, fresh or frozen

Cherries

Peaches

Strawberries, fresh or frozen

Legumes

Great Northern Beans, canned or dry

Kidney Beans, canned or dry

Garbanzo Beans (chickpeas), canned or dry

Shopping Lists continued

Meats

Beef or Pork ribs (unseasoned)	Pork Chops
Beef Roast	Pork Loin, not marinated
Beef round steak (2-3 pounds)	Pork Roast
Chicken legs, thighs, or breasts	Sirloin Steak
Chicken Fry Steaks	Turkey Tenderloin
Chicken, Whole	Turkey, Whole
Lean Hamburger	

Pasta

Couscous	Lasagna noodles
Egg Noodles	Spaghetti noodles
Elbow macaroni	

Spices

Basil	Ground dry mustard
Cayenne pepper	Nutmeg
Chili powder	Oregano
Cream of tartar	Paprika
Crushed rosemary	Parsley
Dried cilantro or fresh if desired	Pepper
Garlic powder	Poppy Seed
Garlic salt	Sage
Ginger	Salt
Ground cinnamon	Thyme
Ground cloves	Vanilla Extract

Shopping Lists continued

Vegetables

Baby carrots
Bell peppers, green
Cabbage
14 oz. canned corn
14 oz. canned green beans
Canned pumpkin
14 oz. canned, unseasoned diced tomatoes
Celery
Frozen broccoli
Frozen carrot chips
Frozen cauliflower
Frozen corn
Frozen green beans
Frozen okra

Frozen peas
Frozen pepper strips
20 oz. frozen spinach
Garlic (you may buy minced garlic in water solution)
Green onion
Leeks
Mushrooms
Potatoes
Shallots
12 oz. tomato paste
Yellow squash
Zucchini

Other

All-purpose flour
Apple juice
Bag of popcorn kernels
Baking powder
Baking soda
Black olives, if desired
Bread
Brown sugar
Butter, salted and unsalted
Cake flour
Canola oil
Club soda
Corn starch
Cornmeal
Eggs

Green olives
Instant brown rice
Light brown sugar
Light corn syrup
Mayonnaise, real
Old-fashioned oats
Olive oil
Powdered sugar
Red hot candies
Shortening, all vegetable
Splenda sweetener
Sugar
White chocolate chips
White vinegar, distilled is best
Whole wheat flour

Recommendations and Allowable Foods

Be sure to check all ingredients before eating any foods.

Beverage Recommendations

Caffeine-free cola
Herbal tea, except flavors that have triggers, i.e. citrus
Caffeine-free root beer
Cranberry, white grape-peach, apple, and other approved fruit juices
Flavored soft drinks not containing citrus or other trigger fruit juices
Diet colas sweetened with Splenda

Breakfast Recommendations

Bagels (not fresh-baked) with cream cheese or Neufchatel cheese, without trigger preservatives
Eggs
Fresh fruit
Pancakes or waffles with syrup
Toast
Whole grain, corn or rice cereals, high in fiber if possible

Salty Snack Recommendations

Corn chips
Crackers (unflavored)
Graham crackers
Melba toast

Natural microwave popcorn
Plain potato chips
Pretzels
Sunflower seeds or pumpkin seeds

Allowable Fruits (Buchholz 220)

Apples
Apricots
Blackberries
Blueberries
Cantaloupe
Cherries
Cranberries
Grapes
Honeydew melon

Kiwi
Mangoes
Nectarines
Peaches
Pears
Strawberries
Watermelon

Recommendations and Allowable Foods continued

Allowable Legumes

Adzuki beans

Bean sprouts

Black beans (turtle beans)

Black-eyed peas

Garbanzo beans (chick-peas)

Great Northern beans

Kidney beans

Pinto beans

Split peas

Allowable Vegetables and Starches (Buchholz 222)

Artichokes

Asparagus

Baked goods-if made with yeast wait 24 hours

Beets

Broccoli

Brussels sprouts

Cabbage

Carrots

Cauliflower

Celery

Cereals without raisins, nuts, or chocolate

Chard

Cucumbers

Chick peas (garbanzos)

Corn

Couscous

Endive

Fennel

Garlic

All lettuces

Mushrooms

Okra

Olives

Parsley

Pasta

Peas (not pods)

Peppers

Polenta

Potatoes

Radicchio

Radishes

Rice (unseasoned)

Spinach

Sprouts

Squash

String Beans

Sweet Potatoes

Tomatoes

Turnips

Yams

Zucchini

Cooking Substitutions

These foods may be used as substitutions in your favorite recipes.

1. Oranges or citrus juice? Use ripe peaches or nectarines instead.

2. Onions or onion powder? Use shallots, leeks, or green onions (spring onions) instead. Or, substitute with garlic powder.

3. Cream of Mushroom or Chicken soup in a can? Use the soup recipes in this book instead.

4. Nuts? Use sunflower seeds or pumpkin seeds instead, if possible (Buchholz 74). (check ingredients in seeds)

5. Soy sauce or teriyaki sauce? Use the recipes in this book instead.

6. Mandarin oranges? Try canned peaches instead.

7. Peanut butter? Use sunflower seed butter instead.

Dietary Triggers to Avoid

For a complete list of dietary triggers, please reference *Heal Your Headache: The 1-2-3*

Program for Taking Charge of Your Pain by David Buchholz, M.D.

1. Caffeine, while it may seem to help your headache in the short term, is actually a migraine trigger in the long term. It causes rebound vasodilation (blood vessel dilation) in your head, leading to worse headaches over time (Buchholz 76). Eventually, your blood vessels need it to stay constricted, and without it you may feel throbbing pain. Caffeine should be avoided at all costs, even within medications.

2. Monosodium Glutamate (MSG) is found not only in many restaurant foods, but also boxed and quick-prepare foods in the supermarket, and even some spices. Avoid poultry seasoning, seasoned salt, bouillons, and other mixed, prepared spices. Croutons and seasoned bread crumbs, flavored chips and snacks, cheap buffet foods, processed meats and veggie burgers, gravies, special sauces, canned or restaurant soups, and even some flavored cheeses contain MSG (74, 79-83). Low-fat and low-calorie foods usually contain monosodium glutamate because the flavor was taken out when the fat and sugar was, so extra flavoring has to be added back in. MSG is a flavor enhancer.

3. Chocolate is a trigger not only due to caffeine, but also because of some natural chemicals found within it (78-79). It is best avoided. White chocolate is fine.

4. Nitrates and nitrites, along with MSG in many cases, can be found in processed meats and fish such as hot dogs, sausage, pepperoni, bologna, salami, many lunch-meats, jerky, some hams, bacon, smoked and pickled meats and fish, caviar, anchovies, and fast food meats (74). These are all best avoided. Any meat that is processed, cured, fermented, marinated, aged or tenderized may give you trouble (74). Any food items, meat or otherwise, containing sulfites should also be avoided. Sulfates are fine.

5. Tyramine can be a very powerful trigger for many, and can be found in a wide variety of foods. Milk is not a trigger, but some dairy products containing tyramine can be triggers. Avoid cheese, yogurt, sour cream and buttermilk (74). You may eat cottage cheese, ricotta cheese, cream cheese, and American cheese from the deli as these are not aged cheeses (74). Other foods that contain tyramine are nuts (seeds are permissible), citrus fruits and juices (pineapples, lemons and limes, grapefruits, oranges, tangerines), onions and onion powder, pea pods, sauerkraut, bananas, raisins, avocados, raspberries, figs, dates, passion fruit and papayas (74). Even some

beans and meat contain tyramine, including beef and chicken livers and wild game, and fava beans, lima beans, navy beans, and lentils (74). Fresh yeast-risen baked goods contain tyramine for the first 24 hours or so after they are baked (87). Generally the more aged a food is, the more tyramine it contains, but yeast does not follow this rule. So, wait one day and then you may enjoy it (87). What can you substitute for some of these foods? Instead of peanut butter try sunflower seed butter. Instead of onions try leeks, shallots, or green onions. Avoid nuts, but enjoy all of the seeds you wish.

6. Fermented items can cause you trouble. Stay away from alcohol and vinegar unless it is clear and distilled. Red wine and dark or heavy drinks can cause problems (85-86). While cooking, use white distilled vinegar.

7. Aspartame, more commonly known as nutrasweet, can be a powerful trigger for some (87). Saccharin can also start the migraine mechanism in some people. Splenda (sucralose) and other sweeteners are generally okay.

8. Tomatoes and tomato-based sauces may be a trigger for some, as well as mushrooms and peas (avoid pea pods) (88). This is due to the high amounts of free glutamate found in these foods (88). This is not to be confused with wheat gluten. Many migraineurs do not have trouble with tomatoes, so leave these in your diet. The diet can feel restrictive enough as it is. If after a couple of months you feel tomatoes might be a problem, eliminate tomatoes, mushrooms and peas. If you don't feel better in a couple of weeks, add them back in.

9. Soy may be a trigger for some, but soy oil is safe (75, 89). Soy oils can be found within many foods, and are commonly used in cooking. Soy, like tomatoes, is not one that causes a problem for many migraine sufferers, but is a trigger for some.

Dietary trigger information is taken from the following source:

Buchholz, David, M.D. Heal Your Headache: The 1-2-3 Program For Taking Charge of Your Pain. New York: Workman, 2002.

Salsa with Tomatoes and Herbs

Appetizers and Beverages

Crab Dip

8 ounces cream cheese or Neufchatel cheese, softened
1 medium leek, chopped
1 clove garlic, finely chopped
¼ cup mayonnaise
2 tablespoons milk or half-and-half
¼ cup apple juice or green olive juice
2 teaspoons sugar or 1 packet Splenda sweetener
1 teaspoon ground dry mustard
1 teaspoon dried parsley flakes
1 teaspoon garlic powder
1 (6 ounce) can crab meat, well drained

Preheat oven to 375 degrees. Mix all ingredients in a medium sized mixing bowl. Spread mixture in a 9-inch pie plate and bake uncovered for 15-20 minutes, or until hot and bubbly. Serve as desired.

Hummus

2 (16 oz.) cans garbanzo beans (chickpeas), drained
2 cloves garlic, chopped
1 teaspoon garlic powder
1 teaspoon cumin
1 teaspoon salt
2 tablespoons olive oil
¼ cup water

Cook all ingredients over low heat in a saucepan until hot. Allow to cool slightly, then place in a food processor or blender and mix until smooth. Serve warm or chilled as desired.

Meatballs (Beef or Turkey)

2 pounds lean ground beef or ground turkey
1 shallot, chopped
2 cloves garlic, minced
2 teaspoons olive oil
6 or 7 large cabbage leaves
1 small package frozen spinach
1 egg
1 teaspoon garlic salt
½ teaspoon pepper

Preheat oven to 400 degrees. Saute shallot and garlic in olive oil for approximately 2 minutes.   Boil spinach and cabbage leaves together for approximately 7 minutes, or until spinach is thawed. Drain and pat dry. Tear cabbage into small pieces. Mix all ingredients together and shape into 1-inch balls. Place on a rack in broiler pan. Bake approximately 20 minutes or until meat is no longer pink in the center and juices run clear.

Roasted Garlic

3 to 4 bulbs garlic
2 teaspoons olive oil for each bulb garlic
Salt and pepper to taste

Preheat oven to 350 degrees. Cut the top of each garlic bulb to expose all cloves and remove most layers of the outer shell. Place cut side up on squares of aluminum foil. Drizzle each bulb with oil and sprinkle with salt and pepper. Wrap each bulb in foil, place in shallow baking pan, and bake for 45 minutes. Squeeze soft garlic out of cloves and spread on toast or crackers to serve.

Salsa with Tomatoes and Herbs

3 to 4 fresh tomatoes, diced or 2 (14 oz) cans diced tomatoes
2 shallots, finely diced
2 cloves garlic, minced
¼ teaspoon cayenne pepper
2 tablespoons distilled white vinegar
1 tablespoon olive oil
1 teaspoon salt, more to taste if needed
1 teaspoon pepper
1/3 cup chopped, fresh cilantro, or 2 teaspoons dried cilantro
½ teaspoon dried oregano, optional

Combine all ingredients and chill to let the flavors set in. Or, blend in a blender for a smoother salsa. Serve as desired. Enjoy!

Spinach Dip

20 ounces frozen chopped spinach
1 (8 oz) package Cream Cheese or Neufchatel cheese, softened
¼ pound butter, melted, or 8 tablespoons olive oil
½ teaspoon sage
½ teaspoon garlic powder
¼ teaspoon oregano
¼ teaspoon basil
½ teaspoon salt
½ teaspoon pepper

Preheat oven to 350 degrees. Spray a 2-quart casserole dish with non-stick spray and set aside. Cook spinach as directed on package and drain thoroughly. Mix all ingredients together in casserole dish. Bake 25 minutes or until hot in center and bubbly around the edges. Serve with corn chips or crackers for a tasty appetizer.

Spinach and Artichoke Dip

1 can artichokes, well drained and chopped (check ingredients)
1 (10 oz.) bag frozen spinach, boiled, drained and patted dry
½ cup mayonnaise
½ cup half and half
2-3 cloves garlic, minced
3-4 slices high-quality American cheese, torn into pieces, optional
2 ounces cream cheese or Neufchatel cheese, cubed
1 teaspoon garlic powder
½ teaspoon salt
Your choice of garnish (chopped tomatoes, green onions, etc.)

Preheat oven to 350 degrees. Mix all ingredients together in a medium size bowl. Spread in a 9-inch pie plate and bake for 25-30 minutes, or until hot and bubbly. Enjoy!

Blue-Strawberry Smoothie

1 cup frozen strawberries
½ cup frozen blueberries
1 cup water
2 teaspoons sugar or 1 packet Splenda sweetener

Combine all ingredients in a blender and blend until smooth. Add more water if needed.

Milkshakes

1 cup milk
4 (½ cup) scoops vanilla ice cream

Blend ingredients together in a blender, on low speed, until smooth. Do not over-blend.

Strawberry Milkshakes

Blend 1 cup fresh strawberries or frozen strawberries with the milk on high speed until smooth. You may add 4 tablespoons strawberry syrup, if desired (check ingredients). Add ice cream and follow directions above.

Root Beer Floats

Vanilla ice cream
Caffeine-free root beer
1 recipe whipped cream topping

Place one scoop of vanilla ice cream in each glass, then fill to the top with root beer. Top with whipped cream topping. Enjoy!

Cornbread Muffins

Breads and Muffins

Blueberry Muffins

2 cups all-purpose flour, or half all-purpose and half whole wheat
3 teaspoons baking powder
½ teaspoon salt
1 cup sugar or Splenda granular
1 large egg, slightly beaten
¾ cup milk
¼ cup melted butter or olive oil
1 cup blueberries, sweetened with 2 tablespoons sugar or Splenda granular plus a sprinkle of cornstarch, and heated in a saucepan over low heat for 5 minutes

Preheat oven to 375 degrees. Spray bottoms of muffin pan with non-stick spray or use paper baking cups. Stir flour, baking powder, salt, and sugar in large bowl. Stir egg, milk, and butter in small bowl until well blended. Pour small bowl mixture into large bowl and stir. Batter will be lumpy. Mix in blueberries. Fill muffin pans 2/3 full. Bake for 20-25 minutes. Remove muffins from pan to a cooling rack.

Apple Cinnamon Muffins

Substitute 2 pared and cored apples for blueberries. Cut into small pieces. Prepare as directed above with the cornstarch. Add 2 teaspoons ground cinnamon to muffin batter before mixing in apples. (add 7 min prep time)

Bread Stuffing

¼ cup butter or olive oil
1 or 2 shallots, chopped
1 stalk celery, chopped
11 to 13 slices bread, cubed and dried (see homemade bread crumbs, but cubed instead of crumbled)
½ tablespoon dried parsley
1 tablespoon dried sage
½ teaspoon garlic powder
1 teaspoon salt
¼ teaspoon pepper
½ cup chicken or turkey stock

In large pan, saute shallots and celery in butter until tender. In large bowl mix bread cubes, parsley, sage, garlic powder, salt and pepper. Add mixture to pan along with stock. Cook until at desired consistency.

Cornbread or Cornbread Muffins

1 cup cornmeal
1 cup all-purpose flour or whole wheat flour (I like to use half of each)
1/3 cup sugar or Splenda granular
2 tsp baking powder
½ tsp salt
1 cup milk
¼ cup melted butter or olive oil
1 large egg

Preheat oven to 400 degrees. Spray 8-inch square pan or muffin pan with non-stick spray and set aside. Combine cornmeal, flour, sugar, baking powder, and salt in a large mixing bowl. Beat milk, butter, and egg in a small bowl. Pour ingredients in small bowl into large bowl and mix all ingredients together. Batter will be lumpy. Pour batter into pan and bake for 25 minutes, or until golden on top.

Homemade Bread Crumbs

Whole wheat or white bread – with or without seasonings

Preheat oven to 200 degrees. Place bread slices on a cookie sheet and bake until hard, but not burnt. Pull apart into pieces or roll into crumbs. For easier crumbs, place cooked bread slices in sandwich bags and mash with hands or rolling pin.

Oatmeal Muffins

1 ½ cups all-purpose flour or whole wheat flour (I like to use half of each)
½ cup packed brown sugar
3 teaspoons baking powder
½ teaspoon salt
¾ cup milk
1 egg, well beaten
4 tablespoons melted butter or olive oil
1 cup old-fashioned oats
1 teaspoon vanilla

Preheat oven to 400 degrees. Spray muffin pans, or line with paper baking cups. Combine dry ingredients, except oatmeal, in a large bowl. Combine wet ingredients and oatmeal in a separate bowl, and stir until well blended. Combine the two mixtures and mix well. Fill each muffin cup 2/3 full with batter. Bake approximately 20 minutes, or until toothpick inserted in the center comes out clean.

Cinnamon oatmeal muffins
Add 3 tablespoons cinnamon to dry mixture before combining.

Raw Baking Ingredients

Cakes and Pies

Angel Food Cake

2 teaspoons vanilla extract
½ teaspoon distilled white vinegar
1 ¾ cups large egg whites (about 12)
¼ teaspoon salt
½ cup granulated sugar
1 ¼ cups powdered sugar
1 cup cake flour

Preheat oven to 350 degrees. Stir vanilla and vinegar together in a small bowl. Set aside. Beat egg whites and salt together in a large bowl until soft peaks form. Mix in the granulated sugar and vanilla mixture until stiff and glossy. Mix powdered sugar and flour together in a sifter and gradually sift over the egg whites while gently folding into the batter. Pour batter into ungreased tube pan, 10 by 4 inches. Break any air pockets. Bake 30-35 minutes or until top springs back when touched. You may also check by inserting a toothpick in the center to make sure it comes out dry. Remove from oven and immediately turn pan upside down onto funnel to cool for about 1 ½ to 2 hours. Remove from pan. Drizzle with vanilla glaze.

Carrot or Apple Cake

2 cups sugar or Splenda granular
1 cup olive oil or shortening
3 large eggs
2 cups cake flour or well sifted all-purpose flour
2 ½ teaspoons cinnamon
¼ teaspoon ginger
¼ teaspoon cloves
¼ teaspoon nutmeg
1 teaspoon baking soda
1 teaspoon baking powder
2 teaspoons vanilla
½ teaspoon salt
2 cups shredded carrots or chopped and peeled apples

Preheat oven to 350 degrees. Grease and lightly flour bottom and sides of 13 by 9 inch cake pan, or two 8- or 9-inch round pans. Mix sugar, oil, and eggs in a large bowl and beat for one minute. Stir in all remaining ingredients except carrots. Beat until smooth. Mixture will be thick. Stir in carrots and pour into pan. Bake rectangular pan 40-45 minutes, round pans 30-35 minutes, or until toothpick inserted in center comes out clean. Remove from oven and cool in the pan(s). Frost with cream cheese frosting.

Cheesecake

1 ½ cups graham cracker crumbs (check ingredients),

1/3 cup melted butter or olive oil

¼ teaspoon cinnamon

¼ teaspoon nutmeg

¼ cup sugar or Splenda granular

5 (8-ounce) packages cream cheese, softened

1 ¾ cups sugar or Splenda granular

¼ teaspoon salt

5 large eggs

2 large egg yolks

1/3 cup heavy whipping cream

2 teaspoons vanilla

Combine graham crumbs, ½ cup butter, cinnamon, nutmeg, and ¼ cup sugar in a bowl and mix well. Butter a 9 inch round spring form pan. Pat the mixture over the bottom one inch up the sides of the pan. Chill. Preheat oven to 325 degrees. Cheesecakes are baked at low temperatures to prevent excess shrinkage. Beat cream cheese, sugar, and salt in a large bowl, with electric mixer, on medium speed until smooth; about 1 minute. Beat in eggs, egg yolks, whipping cream, and vanilla (combine in small bowl first) on low speed until well blended. Pour into crust. Bake approximately one hour, or until center does not shake when cake is gently rocked from side to side. The center may look slightly soft but will set while chilling. Do not insert a toothpick to check for doneness as this could cause the cheesecake to crack. Cool in pan on wire rack 15 minutes, no longer. Run metal spatula along side of cheesecake to loosen. Refrigerate covered immediately, about 9 hours or until chilled. Run metal spatula along side of cheesecake to loosen. Remove side of the pan.

Cheesecake Bars

1 ½ cups graham cracker crumbs (check ingredients)
¼ cup sugar or Splenda granular
½ teaspoon salt
¾ cup butter, softened
2 (8-ounce) packages cream cheese or Neufchatel cheese, softened
3 large eggs
2 teaspoons vanilla
1 ½ cups sugar
Powdered sugar

Preheat oven to 375 degrees. Grease 13 by 9-inch cake pan. Stir graham cracker, sugar, salt and butter together in a medium size mixing bowl until well mixed. Press dough evenly in pan. Beat remaining ingredients except powdered sugar in medium bowl until smooth. Pour over dough. Bake 35 minutes or until edges are light brown and filling is set and appears puffy. Refrigerate until chilled. Sprinkle with powdered sugar just before cutting and serving.

Strawberry Cheesecake Bars

Top with strawberry jam before chilling.

Pound Cake

2 cups sugar or Splenda granular
1 cup butter, softened
2 teaspoons vanilla
5 large eggs
2 1/2 cups all-purpose flour
1 teaspoon baking powder
½ teaspoon salt
1 cup milk

Preheat oven to 350 degrees. Grease and lightly flour two 9 by 5 inch loaf pans. Beat sugar, butter, vanilla, and eggs in a large bowl on high speed for 5 minutes. Mix flour, baking powder, and salt in a separate bowl. Beat into sugar mixture alternately with milk on low speed. Spread in pan and bake for 50-60 minutes, or until toothpick inserted in the center comes out clean. Cool 10 minutes in the pan, then finish cooling on wire rack. Slice and serve.

Pumpkin Cake

1 ¼ cups all-purpose flour
1 ½ cups sugar or Splenda granular
2 teaspoons baking powder
1 teaspoon salt
2 teaspoons cinnamon
¼ teaspoon nutmeg
¼ teaspoon cloves
¼ teaspoon ginger
2/3 cup milk
½ cup shortening
2 eggs
1 cup pumpkin

Preheat oven to 350 degrees. Spray a 9 by 13 inch baking dish with non-stick spray and set aside. Combine all ingredients in a large mixing bowl. Mix until smooth. Pour in baking dish and bake for 30 minutes or until toothpick inserted in center comes out clean. Cool in pan. Frost with Whipped Frosting.

Sponge Cake

5 large eggs, separated
½ teaspoon salt
1 cup + ½ cup sugar or Splenda granular
3 to 4 tablespoons water
2 teaspoons vanilla extract
1 ¼ cups cake flour, sifted
2 teaspoons baking powder

Preheat oven to 350 degrees. In a large bowl, beat egg whites and salt to soft mounds. Add ½ cup sugar and beat to stiff points. In another large bowl, beat egg yolks and vanilla until the yolks are pale and thick. Mix in remaining ingredients, including the remaining sugar. Bake for 40 to 50 minutes in an ungreased tube pan. Cool for 10 minutes upright, then turn pan upside down on a funnel to cool completely.

White Cake

2 ¾ cups cake flour
3 teaspoons baking powder
½ teaspoon salt
1 2/3 cups sugar or Splenda granular
2/3 cups shortening or butter
1 ¼ cups milk
2 teaspoons vanilla extract
5 large egg whites

Preheat oven to 350 degrees. Grease and flour a 9 by 13 inch baking dish or two 9-inch round pans. Set aside. Sift four, baking soda, salt together and set aside. Cream butter and sugar together. Combine and beat all ingredients except egg whites in large bowl on high speed for two minutes. Beat in egg whites on high speed for two minutes. Bake 9 by 13 inch baking dish approximately 40 minutes, and 9-inch rounds 30 minutes, or until toothpick inserted in center comes out clean. Cool rectangle in pan. Cool rounds 10 minutes, then remove to wire rack to cool completely. Frost with Buttercream Frosting.

Yellow Cake

2 ½ cups cake flour
1 ¾ cups sugar or Splenda granular
2/3 cup shortening
1 ¼ cups milk
3 teaspoons baking powder
½ teaspoon salt
2 teaspoons vanilla
3 large eggs

Preheat oven to 350 degrees. Grease and lightly flour a 9 by 13 inch baking dish, or two 9-inch round pans. Beat all ingredients on high speed for 2 ½ to 3 minutes. Pour into pans. Bake 9 by 13 inch baking dish for approximately 40 minutes, and 9-inch rounds 30 minutes, or until toothpick inserted in center comes out clean. Cool rectangle in pan. Cool rounds 10 minutes, then remove to wire rack to cool completely.

Poppy Seed Cake

Stir in ¼ cup poppy seeds before pouring into pans.

Zucchini Cake

3 eggs
1 ½ cups sugar or Splenda granular
1 ½ teaspoons vanilla
½ cup olive oil
2 cups flour
3 teaspoons baking powder
1 teaspoon cinnamon
½ teaspoon salt
¾ cup milk
1 ½ cups shredded raw zucchini

Preheat oven to 350 degrees. Spray a 9 by 13 inch baking dish with non-stick spray. Beat eggs, sugar, vanilla, and oil together for approximately one minute. Add flour, baking powder, cinnamon, salt, and milk. Mix until smooth. Fold zucchini into batter. Bake for 45 to 45 minutes. Cool in pan. Frost with Cream Cheese Frosting.

Apple Pie

1 recipe pie crust
1 tablespoon cornstarch
2 tablespoons melted butter or olive oil
1 ½ teaspoons ground cinnamon
½ cup sugar or Splenda granular
½ teaspoon ground nutmeg
4 medium thinly sliced and peeled apples

Preheat oven to 425 degrees. Prepare crust. Mix all ingredients except apples in a bowl. Stir in apples. Follow instructions in pie crust recipe for lining and filling pie crusts. Bake 40 to 50 minutes or until crust is golden brown and pie is bubbly. Serve cool or warm as desired.

Peach Pie

Substitute fresh peaches for apples.

Blueberry Pie

Substitute 3 cups blueberries for apples and omit cinnamon.

Cherry Pie

Omit cinnamon. Substitute 3 cups cherries for apples. Increase sugar to 1 cup and cornstarch to 2 tablespoons.

Fresh Apple Crisp or Cobbler

1 tablespoon corn starch

2 teaspoons ground cinnamon

½ cup sugar or Splenda granular

6 medium apples, peeled and sliced thin

½ stick melted butter or ¼ cup olive oil

Preheat oven to 375 degrees. Mix cornstarch, cinnamon, and sugar in large saucepan. Stir in apples. Cook and stir until boiling, then boil and stir for one minute. Add butter and cook until melted. Pour into a greased 9 by 13 inch baking dish. Top with topping and bake 25-30 minutes or until cobbler topping is lightly browned.

Crisp Topping

1 stick melted butter or olive oil

6 cups old fashioned oats

2 tsp ground cinnamon

½ cup sugar or Splenda granular

Stir all ingredients together and spread on top of apples.

Cobbler Topping

4 tablespoons shortening or butter, softened

1 cup all-purpose flour or whole wheat flour

2 tablespoons sugar or Splenda granular

1 tablespoon baking powder

½ teaspoon salt

¼ cup milk

Combine all ingredients together except milk using pastry blender until mixture resembles fine crumbs. You may do this with fingertips also. Stir in the milk. Drop by spoonful onto apples.

Peach Crisp or Cobbler

Substitute peaches for apples

Blueberry Crisp or Cobbler

Substitute 4 cups blueberries for apples and omit cinnamon.

Cherry Crisp or Cobbler

Omit Cinnamon. Substitute 4 cups cherries for apples. Increase sugar to 1 cup and cornstarch to 2 tablespoons.

Pumpkin Pie

1 recipe pie crust
2 large eggs
¾ cup sugar or Splenda granular
1 ½ teaspoons ground cinnamon
½ teaspoon salt
½ teaspoon ground ginger
¼ teaspoon ground cloves
¼ teaspoon nutmeg
1 (16 ounce) can pumpkin
1 (12 ounce) can evaporated milk
¼ cup milk

Preheat oven to 425 degrees. Prepare crust. Beat all ingredients in a large bowl with an electric mixer until well blended. Fill pie plate. Bake 15 minutes at 425 degrees. Reduce oven temperature to 325 degrees. Bake 45 minutes longer or until toothpick inserted in center comes out clean. Refrigerate approximately 4 hours. Top with Whipped Cream Topping.

Pie Crust

1¾ cups all-purpose flour
½ cup shortening
¼ teaspoon salt
4 tablespoons cold water + 2 teaspoons water, if needed

Cut shortening into flour and salt until mixture resembles coarse crumbs. Stir in only enough water to hold dough together. Knead lightly to mix well. Lightly flour a cutting board or wax paper. Shape pastry ball into flattened round, 1/8 inch thick, by using a floured rolling pin. Roll dough onto rolling pin and unroll onto pie plate pressing gently with fingers so there are no air bubbles. Trim the edge with a knife. Place the filling in the pie. Form the top crust of strips, designs, or of rolled dough in which a few cuts have been made to allow steam to escape. Moisten the edge of the lower crust, and press the two crusts together with fingers or fork.

Frostings and Toppings

Buttercream Frosting

6 cups powdered sugar
2/3 cups butter, softened
6 teaspoons vanilla
4 tablespoons milk

Mix all ingredients in a medium size bowl. Beat with electric mixer until smooth and spreadable.

Caramel Topping

¼ cup butter, melted
½ cup packed brown sugar
2 tablespoons milk

Mix all ingredients together in a pan and heat over low heat, stirring constantly, until smooth.

Cream Cheese Frosting

2 (8-ounce) packages cream cheese, softened
½ cup butter, softened
2 teaspoons milk or water
3 teaspoons vanilla
3 ½ cups powdered sugar

Beat all ingredients together with electric mixer until smooth and spreadable.

Streusel Topping

½ cup powdered sugar
2 tablespoons butter, softened
1 teaspoon ground cinnamon

Mix all ingredients until mixture resembles coarse crumbs.

Vanilla Glaze

1/3 cup butter
2 ½ cups powdered sugar
3 teaspoons vanilla extract
3 tablespoons hot water

Melt butter in medium saucepan. Add remaining ingredients and stir until thick.

Whipped Cream Frosting

1 cup evaporated milk
½ cup powdered sugar
1 stick butter, softened
3 egg yolks

Blend all ingredients and cook over low heat until thick; approximately 10-15 minutes.

Whipped Cream Topping

1 cup heavy whipping cream
4 tablespoons powdered sugar

Beat in chilled bowl on high speed until stiff.

Oatmeal Cookies

Cookies and Candies

Pumpkin Cookies

2/3 cup butter or shortening

1 ½ cups packed brown sugar

2 large eggs

1 cup pumpkin

2 teaspoons vanilla

2 cups sifted all-purpose flour or 2 ¼ cups cake flour

3 teaspoons baking powder

1 teaspoon salt

¼ teaspoon ginger

¼ teaspoon cloves

¼ teaspoon nutmeg

1 teaspoon cinnamon

Preheat oven to 375 degrees. Cream together butter and sugar. Beat remaining ingredients into the butter mixture. Drop by the teaspoonful approximately 2 inches apart onto greased cookie sheet. Bake for 8 to 12 minutes. Cool on cooling racks. (Thanks for the recipe Grandma)

Snickerdoodles

1 cup shortening, softened

1 ½ cups sugar

2 eggs

2 2/3 cups flour

1 teaspoon baking soda

1 teaspoon salt

2 teaspoons cream of tartar (cream of tartar may cause headaches for some, optional)

2 tablespoons sugar or Splenda granular + 2 tablespoons cinnamon, mixed

Preheat oven to 400 degrees. Cream all ingredients together except sugar and cinnamon mixture. Roll the dough into balls, and then roll in the sugar and cinnamon mixture. Place two inches apart on ungreased baking sheet and bake for 7 to 9 minutes. Cool on cooling racks.

Sugar Cookies

1 cup sugar or Splenda granular
½ cup shortening
½ cup butter
1 egg
1 teaspoon vanilla
2 cups flour
½ teaspoon baking soda
½ teaspoon baking powder
½ teaspoon salt

Preheat oven to 350 degrees. In a large mixing bowl, cream together sugar, shortening and butter. Add egg and vanilla and mix well. In a small bowl, combine flour, baking soda, baking powder, and salt. Gradually beat into the large bowl. Roll into small balls. Roll the balls in sugar. Bake on a greased cookie sheet for about 9-10 minutes, or until lightly browned. Cool on cooling racks.

White Chocolate Chip Oatmeal Cookies

1 ½ cups flour
1 teaspoon baking soda
½ teaspoon salt
1 cup shortening or butter, softened
½ cup sugar or Splenda granular
1 cup packed brown sugar
1 teaspoon cinnamon
1 teaspoon vanilla
½ teaspoon water
2 large eggs
1 package white chocolate chips
3 cups uncooked old-fashioned oats

Preheat oven to 375 degrees. Sift together flour, baking soda and salt. Combine shortening, sugar, brown sugar, cinnamon, vanilla, and water in a separate bowl. Beat in eggs. Add flour mixture and beat all ingredients together. Stir in white chocolate chips and oats. Drop by teaspoonful on ungreased cookie sheet. Bake for 10 to 12 minutes and cool on wire rack. Do not overcook as the cookies will be too crispy.

Caramels

1 cup brown sugar
1 cup granulated sugar
½ cup butter, softened
2 cups heavy whipping cream
¾ cup light corn syrup
1 teaspoon vanilla

Grease 8- or 9-inch square baking pan with butter. Heat all ingredients to boiling in large, heavy-bottomed pan over medium heat, stirring constantly. Cook to 242-248 degrees on candy thermometer or until a small amount dropped in really cold water forms a firm ball that holds its shape until pressed between two fingers. Add vanilla and immediately spread in pan. Allow to cool. Cut into squares and wrap individually in waxed paper.

Mints

3 cups powdered sugar
1 cup boiling water
12 drops peppermint oil or wintergreen oil
Blue or green food coloring

Boil sugar and water in a pan until mixture forms a soft ball when dropped into a bowl of cold water, or reaches 234-240 degrees on a candy thermometer. Add peppermint oil and blue food coloring. Remove from heat and beat until thickened. Drop from a spoon into thin patties on wax paper and allow to cool.

Popcorn

Popcorn kernels
Canola oil, organic (expeller pressed) canola oil, or olive oil
Salt to taste

Cover the bottom of a large, heavy-bottomed pan with canola oil. A dutch oven works really well. Put two to three kernels in, turn the heat to medium, and wait for them to pop. When just one kernel pops, the oil is ready. Add just enough kernels to cover the bottom of the pan. Cook, moving pan quickly from side to side, until the popping slows. Quickly remove to a large mixing bowl so popcorn does not burn. Dust lightly with salt and enjoy.

Popcorn Balls

½ cup sugar or brown sugar
¼ cup butter
½ cup light corn syrup
¼ teaspoon salt
1 teaspoon vanilla
8 cups popped popcorn
½ cup candies of your choice

Cook popcorn as directed on previous page but omit the salt. In dutch oven, heat all ingredients except popcorn and candies to boiling, stirring constantly, over medium-high heat. Boil for two minutes while continuing to stir, but do not overheat. If mixture starts to turn white, it has been cooked too long. Remove from heat. Stir in popcorn until well coated. Allow to cool slightly, then stir in candy pieces. Coat hands with butter or cool water. Shape into balls and allow to cool on wax paper.

Caramel Popcorn

10 cups popcorn recipe, unsalted
1 cup packed light brown sugar
¼ cup granulated sugar
½ cup butter
¼ cup light corn syrup
½ teaspoon salt
1 ½ teaspoons baking soda

Pour popcorn in a greased 9 by 13 inch baking dish. Cook sugars, butter, corn syrup and salt in a medium heavy-bottomed saucepan until they reach 255 to 260 degrees on a candy thermometer, or until a small amount of the mixture pressed between two fingers forms a hard ball that holds its shape but is pliable. Pour in the baking soda and stir until foamy. Immediately pour over the popcorn and stir until well coated. Cool for approximately one hour, then break apart and enjoy. Store in a closed container.

Cinnamon Popcorn

10 cups unsalted popcorn (above)
½ cup butter
1 ½ cups cinnamon imperials
½ teaspoon salt

Melt butter, cinnamon imperials, and salt in a pan over medium heat. Spread popcorn in a 9 by 13 inch baking dish. Pour cinnamon mixture over popcorn and stir well before mixture cools. Allow to cool completely and enjoy. Store in a closed container.

Vanilla Ice Cream (for ice cream maker)

6 eggs
3 ¾ cups sugar or Splenda granular
5 tablespoons vanilla
Milk

Beat together eggs and sugar. Add vanilla and enough milk to fill freezer can. Follow instructions for your ice cream freezer.

Vanilla Pudding

½ cup sugar or Splenda granular
3 tablespoons cornstarch
1/8 teaspoon salt
2 cups milk
2 large egg yolks, slightly beaten
3 tablespoons butter or olive oil
3 teaspoons vanilla

Mix sugar, cornstarch, and salt in medium saucepan. Stir constantly over medium heat, while gradually adding milk, until mixture thickens. Boil and stir two minutes. Remove from heat. Beat egg yolks, butter and vanilla in a separate bowl. Gradually stir them into the pan mixture. Place the pan back over the heat, and boil and stir the mixture for two minutes. Remove from heat, place in a serving dish, and cover and refrigerate until ready to serve.

White Chocolate Pretzels

2 tablespoons butter or shortening
12 (1 ounce) squares white baking chocolate
1 (15 ounce) bag mini pretzels (check ingredients)
Candy topping, if desired

In medium mixing bowl, combine butter and chocolate. Melt in microwave for 30 seconds at a time until hot and smooth, but do not burn. Dip pretzels in chocolate and lay on wax paper to cool. If you desire candy toppings, sprinkle it on before the chocolate cools.

Raw Ingredients, Milk and Herbal Tea

Eggs and Breakfast Items

Custard

12 large eggs
1 ½ cups sugar
5 cups milk
4 teaspoons vanilla
½ teaspoon nutmeg
¼ teaspoon salt

Preheat oven to 350 degrees. Beat ingredients in a large mixing bowl until fully blended. Pour into a 9 by 13 inch baking dish and bake for 55 to 60 minutes, or until custard has set and a toothpick inserted in the center comes out clean. Chill completely, then cut in squares and serve. Immediately refrigerate any leftovers.

Optional Caramel Topping:
2 tablespoons butter
1 cup sugar
Heat butter and sugar over medium-low heat until smooth and browned. Pour over custard squares and enjoy.

Deviled Eggs

4 to 6 hard boiled eggs
3 tablespoons mayonnaise
¼ teaspoon ground dry mustard
¼ teaspoon pepper
1/8 teaspoon green olive juice
Salt to taste

Cut eggs in half lengthwise and scoop yolks out with a fork. Mash yolks and all other ingredients together in a bowl. Stuff equal amounts of filling into the hollow part of each egg white. Top with olives, parsley, or paprika if desired.

Hard-boiled Eggs

Place eggs in cold water reaching at least one inch above eggs to avoid cracking. Heat to boiling; remove from heat. Cover and let stand 18 minutes. Immediately cool in cold water to prevent further cooking. Tap and crack egg shell, then roll in hands to loosen shell from egg. For ease, peel in cold water.

Scrambled Eggs

1 tablespoon butter
4 to 6 eggs
¼ cup milk (or water if desired)
Salt and pepper to taste

Beat all ingredients except butter with fork or whisk until well blended. Melt 1 tablespoon butter in frying pan until a few drops of water sprinkled in pan sizzle. Pour mixture into pan. Stir and separate (not too frequently as the eggs will be dry) until eggs are done but still moist.

Western Omelet

1 tablespoon butter
3 eggs, beaten
¼ cup fully cooked ham, diced (check ingredients)
2 tablespoons shallot, leek, or green onion, chopped fine
2 tablespoons bell pepper, chopped fine

Melt butter in an 8- or 9-inch skillet over medium-high heat. Tilt to coat bottom completely. Pour eggs into skillet and stir with fork until thickened. Let sit for about 15 seconds to lightly brown bottom of omelet. Center may still be a little runny. Sprinkle toppings into omelet. Fold to center with fork while jerking skillet to loosen egg if needed. Tilt skillet to allow loose egg to run out and cook. When completely done, turn omelet onto plate upside down.

French Toast

3 large eggs
½ cup milk
1 teaspoon sugar or Splenda granular
½ teaspoon vanilla
Dash of salt
6-8 slices of bread
1-2 tablespoons butter

Beat all ingredients except bread and butter with fork or whisk until smooth. Heat skillet over medium-low heat until drops of water sprinkled on the pan sizzle and jump around. Melt butter on pan. Dip bread into egg mixture and cook each side until golden brown.

Pancakes

1 large egg, whisked
1 ½ cups all-purpose or whole wheat flour (I like to use half of each)
1 ¼ cups milk
2 tablespoons sugar
2 tablespoons olive or canola oil
3 ½ teaspoons baking powder
¼ teaspoon salt
Butter

Beat all ingredients, except butter, in medium size mixing bowl until smooth. For thinner pancakes, use more milk. For thicker pancakes, use less milk. Heat skillet or griddle to medium-low or medium heat. Melt butter on skillet before each pancake. Poor slightly less than ¼ cupful of batter for each pancake on skillet, and cook until edges lift from the pan or pancake bubbles a little on top. Turn and cook until the other side is golden brown.

Blueberry pancakes

Stir ½ to 1 cup fresh blueberries, slightly sweetened if desired, into batter. Frozen blueberries, thawed, may be used also.

Maple and Brown Sugar Oatmeal

1 serving plain instant oats
2 teaspoons packed brown sugar
2 teaspoons maple syrup
1/8 teaspoon salt, optional

Prepare oatmeal as directed on package, but add other ingredients before cooking.

Tuna Salad

Fish

Baked Cajun Tilapia

4 tilapia fillets
3 tablespoons melted butter or olive oil
Sprinkle with Cajun seasoning recipe

Preheat oven to 375 degrees. Sprinkle tilapia with Cajun seasoning on both sides. Arrange fillets in a 9 by 13 inch baking dish. Drizzle with melted butter. Bake uncovered for 15 to 20 minutes or until fish flakes easily with a fork.

Broiled Fish

4 small salmon or other fatty fish
3 to 4 tablespoons butter, melted
Salt and pepper to taste
Other spices, if desired

Preheat the broiler with oven rack in second from top position. Brush both sides of fish with butter and dust with salt and pepper. Place fish on broiler pan rack and broil 5 minutes. Brush both sides with butter again and place fish on the opposite side. Broil approximately 5 minutes longer or until fish flakes easily with fork. *For fish fillets (non-fatty fish), cut into serving size pieces and do not turn.

Crab Cakes

2 cans crab meat, drained
1 ½ cups homemade bread crumbs or plain bread crumbs (check ingredients)
4 tablespoons melted butter or olive oil
1 teaspoon ground dry mustard
½ teaspoon salt
¼ teaspoon pepper
½ teaspoon dried parsley
1 large egg
3 tablespoons mayonnaise
Canola or olive oil, or shortening

Stir all ingredients together except oil in a mixing bowl. Shape mixture into patties. Heat 1 inch of oil in skillet over medium heat. Fry patties until golden brown on both sides.

Fried Fish

1 pound lean fish fillets
Salt and pepper to taste
2 large eggs, whisked
Cornmeal or all-purpose flour (I like to use a mixture)
Canola or olive oil

Heat oil in large skillet over medium heat. Cut fillets into serving size pieces and dust with salt and pepper. Dip fish into egg and coat with cornmeal or flour. Fry fish approximately 8-10 minutes, turning halfway through, or until golden brown and fish flakes easily with fork. Enjoy!

Fried Shrimp

1 pound fresh or frozen deveined shrimp with tails, thawed
Canola or olive oil
2 to 3 large eggs, whisked
½ cup all-purpose flour
1 cup bread crumbs (homemade, or check ingredients), or 1 cup cornmeal
1 teaspoon salt
½ teaspoon pepper

Heat about 3 inches of oil (or enough to cover shrimp to the top) in dutch oven to 325 degrees. Mix flour, bread crumbs, salt and pepper. Coat shrimp with flour mixture, dip into eggs, then coat with flour mixture again. Fry in oil for about two minutes, or until golden brown. *For oysters or clams, follow the same instructions, just substitute drained, shucked oysters or clams for the shrimp.

Garlic Butter Shrimp

1 pound fresh or frozen deveined shrimp with tails, thawed
4 tablespoons melted butter or olive oil
Garlic salt

Preheat oven to 375 degrees. Move oven rack to second from top position. Place shrimp in a 9 by 13 inch baking dish, spread apart, and drizzle with butter. Sprinkle with garlic salt. Bake for 10 minutes, stir with spoon, and bake for 8 to 10 minutes more. Enjoy!

Seasoned Salmon

4 to 6 salmon fillets weighing about 6 ounces each
1 teaspoon garlic salt
1 teaspoon dried thyme
½ leek, chopped fine
¼ teaspoon dried oregano
2 teaspoons honey, optional
2 cups water

Bring water and spices to a boil in large skillet. Place salmon fillets in water. Heat to boiling and reduce heat to low. Simmer about 15 minutes, cooking each side, until salmon flakes easily with a fork.

Tuna Salad

1 (6 ounce) can tuna in water (not preserved in hydrolyzed protein)
1 hard-boiled egg, chopped
½ medium apple chopped
3 tablespoons mayonnaise
¼ tsp ground dry mustard

Mix tuna, mayonnaise, and mustard together with a fork. Stir in egg and apples and enjoy.

Chicken Tetrazzini

Meats and Main Dishes

Barbecue Chicken Sandwiches

1 pound leftover chicken, shredded or torn into bite size pieces
1 recipe Barbecue Sauce

Preheat oven to 350 degrees. Stir chicken and sauce together in a baking dish. Bake for 12-15 minutes. Serve on whole wheat bread or hamburger buns. Enjoy!

Brown Sugar Chicken

3 to 4 pound 100% natural whole chicken
brown sugar
salt and pepper to taste
any other spices you prefer
butter

Preheat the oven to 375 degrees. Remove giblets from inside the chicken. Remove skin by pulling from front to back and ending at the feet. Rinse chicken, including body cavity. Place breast side up in roasting pan. Sprinkle with salt and pepper, including body cavity. Sprinkle with brown sugar and rub into chicken to make it stick. Drizzle butter over brown sugar. Bake for 1 ½-2 hours, or until a meat thermometer placed in between thigh and breast reaches 180 degrees. Do not overcook as the chicken will be dry. Carve and serve. Note: You may also use chicken legs or thighs, but be sure to skin them before cooking.

Chicken and Biscuits

1 Cream of Chicken Soup recipe made with no water
1 package frozen mixed carrots, peas, green beans and corn
2 large eggs
3 tablespoons milk
½ cup all-purpose flour or wheat flour
½ tablespoon sugar
1 tablespoon olive oil or canola oil
2 teaspoons baking powder
1/8 teaspoon salt

Preheat oven to 375 degrees. Stir soup recipe and vegetables together in a square casserole dish sprayed with non-stick cooking spray. Mix remaining ingredients together in a medium mixing bowl to make biscuit dough. Drop by heaping spoonfuls over soup mixture to form biscuits. Bake approximately 30-35 minutes, or until biscuits are golden brown and casserole is hot and bubbly.

Chicken and Rice Casserole

1 recipe cream of chicken soup, but make with no water and only ¾ teaspoon salt
1 ½ cups cooked brown rice
1 cup mushrooms
1 (14 oz.) can green beans
1 (14 oz.) can corn

Preheat oven to 350 degrees. Mix all ingredients and pour into 2-quart casserole dish. Bake uncovered 40-45 minutes or until hot and bubbly.

Tuna Casserole

Do not add chicken to soup recipe. Omit rice and green beans. Add 1 small package frozen peas and two cans tuna, drained. Top with crushed plain potato chips or 1 recipe Fried Onion Topping, and cover before baking.

Chicken and Spinach Salad

8-10 cups baby spinach leaves, or use half lettuce if you wish
2-3 apples, thinly sliced, or one small can peaches, drained
2 small cooked chicken breasts, sliced
¼ cup sunflower seeds
1 recipe Italian dressing

Toss all ingredients except dressing together in a large salad bowl. Garnish with dressing as desired.

Chicken Fried Steak with Mashed Potatoes and Gravy

2 to 4 cube steaks
¼ cup plus 3 tablespoons flour
3 tablespoons shortening, butter, or olive oil
1 ½ cups milk plus ¼ cup milk
4 to 6 medium potatoes
2 to 3 tablespoons butter, softened
Salt and pepper to taste

The Steaks

Push flour into the steak with the tips of your fingers. Sprinkle with salt and pepper. Heat the shortening in a large skillet over high heat. Cook the steaks until golden brown, about three minutes on each side. Set aside and keep warm.

The Gravy

Remove all but two tablespoons of fat from the skillet. Add 3 tablespoons flour and blend together with a fork over low heat. Add 1 ½ cups milk gradually, stirring constantly. Turn heat to medium and continue to stir bringing gravy just to a boil. Remove to a serving dish.

The Potatoes

Wash potatoes. Peel them, if desired, and cut into about one inch square pieces. Place in boiling water. Boil until corners of potatoes start to fade and potatoes can easily be cut in half with a fork. Drain water. Add ¼ cup milk, salt and pepper, and 2 to 3 tablespoons butter. Mix with an electric mixer until blended. Add more milk if potatoes are too dry.

Chicken Pot Pie

1 recipe pie crust
1 recipe cream of chicken soup
¼ package frozen peas
¼ package frozen carrots
¼ package frozen corn
1 large potato, diced

Preheat oven to 425 degrees. Place bottom crust in 9-inch pie plate. Boil potatoes and carrots together for 5 minutes. Drain. Combine soup, peas, corn, potatoes and carrots in a mixing bowl, and then spread on top of bottom crust. Place top crust on and seal. Cut slits in top crust. Bake 35 minutes or until golden brown.

Chicken or Turkey Tetrazzini

7 ounces cooked spaghetti noodles
1 pound cooked chicken or turkey meat, cut into bite size pieces
1 cup hot chicken or turkey stock (you may add water to it if you don't have enough)
2 tablespoons butter or olive oil
3 tablespoons flour
1/3 cup milk
¼ teaspoon paprika
Salt to taste
1 cup cooked peas, corn, or sauteed mushrooms if desired

Preheat oven to 400 degrees. Spray a 2 quart casserole dish with non-stick spray. Set aside. Melt the butter in a heavy bottomed pan. Add flour and stir over moderate heat until smooth. Stir constantly for 2 more minutes. Slowly add chicken stock while continuing to stir. Bring to a boil. Lower heat and stir for 2 more minutes. Add milk, salt, and paprika and heat thoroughly, but do not boil. Stir sauce, spaghetti, meat and peas together and pour into the baking dish. Bake for 30-35 minutes and enjoy.

Grandma's Chicken and Dumplins

2 cups flour
Dash of salt
1 teaspoon baking powder
2 eggs
About 1 ½ cups water
2 recipes chicken stock
1 pound cooked chicken, cut or shredded into bite size pieces
salt and pepper to taste
water, if needed, to make more broth
1 recipe mashed potatoes

Combine flour, dash of salt, baking powder, eggs, and approximately 1 ½ cups water, or as much water as needed, until dough forms. Roll out dough to about ½ inch thick and cut into strips. Bring chicken stock to a boil. Place the strips in boiling broth away from each other and cook until done. Add the chicken, salt and pepper and heat thoroughly. Water may be added to the broth to make more, but do not add too much or you will lose flavor. Serve over mashed potatoes and enjoy! (Thanks for the recipe Grandma)

Herb Tomato-Baked Pork Chops with Peppers and Squash

2 shallots, chopped
4 pork chops
1 can diced tomatoes
½ recipe Italian salad dressing + ½ cup water
½ teaspoon garlic powder
1 green pepper, cut into bite size pieces
1 yellow squash, cut into bit size rounds

Preheat oven to 400 degrees. Combine all ingredients except pork chops in a large mixing bowl. Spoon a small amount of sauce into a 9 by 13 inch baking pan and spread out evenly to coat the bottom of the dish. Place pork chops into the pan and cover with combined ingredients. Bake approximately one hour, or until meat is no longer pink in the center and vegetables are tender.

Roasted Whole Chicken or Turkey and Stock

3 to 5 pound 100% natural whole chicken
Salt and pepper to taste

Preheat the oven to 375 degrees. Remove giblets from inside the chicken. Rinse chicken with water, including body cavity. Place chicken breast side up in roasting pan. Sprinkle with salt and pepper, including body cavity, if desired. Bake for approximately 2 hours, or until a meat thermometer placed in between thigh and breast reaches 180 degrees. Do not let thermometer touch the bone. Remove juice from pan every 30 minutes after the first hour of baking. **Do not throw away the juice from the chicken (chicken stock). Refrigerate stock overnight to separate the fat from the broth. Skim fat off the top before using. Save for as long as three days to use in other recipes or freeze for future use.**
*You can also make broth by boiling the whole chicken in a dutch oven. Remove giblets and rinse chicken as instructed above. Place chicken in 4 cups cold water along with diced celery, carrots, shallots, parsley, salt, and pepper. Heat to boiling. Skim foam from the top of the broth. Simmer and cover over low heat for 45 minutes to one hour. Strain the vegetables from the broth and discard. Refrigerate until fat is separated from the stock. **For turkey, preheat oven to 350 degrees and bake for 2-3 hours for a small turkey (6-10 lbs), 3-4 hours for a medium turkey (12-16 lbs), 5-5 ½ hours for a large turkey (16-24 lbs), or until a meat thermometer reaches 180 degrees.**

Vegetable Broth

Vegetable broth can be made by combining the following ingredients in a pot, bringing to a boil, then simmering for one hour. Then, strain broth and discard vegetables. Use 6 cups water, 2 shallots chopped, 4-5 cloves garlic chopped, 1 teaspoon parsley, bell peppers chopped, carrots chopped, celery chopped, leeks chopped, potatoes peeled and chopped, zucchini chopped, 1 teaspoon dried basil, 1 teaspoon dried thyme leaves, 1 teaspoon salt, ½ teaspoon pepper, anything else you desire.

Rosemary Pork *Very Good!*

1 ½ -2 pound boneless pork roast or pork shoulder, sliced /6 boneless pork loin chops
2 shallots, chopped
2 cups mushrooms, sliced
1 (14 oz.) can diced tomatoes
1 teaspoon dried rosemary
1 teaspoon salt
½ teaspoon pepper
1 cup water

1 cup Rice } saute over med-high
¼ cup Butter } heat until rice is golden brown. Then
Add to crockpot sprayed with Pam.

Combine all ingredients in dutch oven and simmer 1 ½ -2 hours or until tender and meat is no longer pink in the center.
Add all other ingredients + cook on high for 2-2½ hours.

Seasoned Pork Chops or Chicken Breasts

3 to 4 pork chops or chicken breasts
Garlic salt
Pepper
Water or chicken stock

Lightly sprinkle meat with garlic salt and pepper on each side. Place in large skillet on medium heat. Lightly cook both sides. Add enough water to cover the bottom of the pan. Cover and cook until meat is no longer pink in the middle and juices run clear. Turn meat and add water as needed while cooking.

Spicy Chicken and Peppers

1 ½ pounds cut-up broiler-fryer chicken
¼ cup chopped fresh parsley
½ teaspoon cayenne pepper
2 cloves garlic, finely chopped
2 tablespoons olive oil
1 bag frozen pepper strips
1 teaspoon dried basil
½ cup chicken stock
1 teaspoon salt

Preheat oven to 375 degrees. Mix parsley, pepper, and garlic. Heat oil in skillet over medium heat. Cook parsley mixture in oil for 2 minutes. Add chicken and cook for about ten minutes. Place chicken in ungreased 9 by 13 inch baking dish. Arrange pepper strips around chicken and sprinkle with basil. Add chicken stock to skillet and bring to a boil to loosen particles on bottom of skillet. Immediately pour over chicken and peppers and sprinkle with salt. Cover and bake for 45 minutes to one hour, or until chicken is no longer pink in the center. Turn chicken halfway through.

Broiled Pork or Turkey Tenderloin with Herbs

2 tenderloins
Olive oil
Mixed dried spices, such as thyme, sage, rosemary, oregano,
        garlic salt, basil, pepper

Preheat the broiler. Lightly brush meat on both sides with olive oil. Then, sprinkle the mixed spices on the tenderloins. Cook tenderloins on a broiler pan with oven rack in the second from top position. Cook for about 6 minutes, turn and cook another 6 minutes, or until meat is no longer pink in the middle. Slice and serve. Turkey may need to cook a little longer.

Ribs

3 to 4 pounds beef or pork ribs
1 recipe barbecue sauce

Preheat oven to 350 degrees. Place ribs in a 9 by 13 inch baking dish. Cover with sauce. Cover and bake 2 ½ to 3 hours or until tender and meat starts to shrink on the bone. Spoon sauce over ribs again before the last 30 minutes of baking.

Roast with Potatoes and Carrots

1 lean beef or pork roast of any size
1 cup water
1 shallot, chopped
6 medium peeled and cut carrots
4 potatoes, peeled if desired, and cubed
Salt and pepper to taste

Brown all sides of roast over medium heat in dutch oven. Add water and reduce heat to simmer. Add shallot. Cover and simmer over low heat 1 to 1 ½ hours. Add potatoes, carrots and salt and pepper and cook for one more hour.

Gravy:
Broth from roast plus enough water to measure 2 cups
½ cup cold water
¼ cup all-purpose flour

Skim excess fat from broth in Dutch oven. Stir cold water and flour together with a fork until there are no lumps. Gradually stir into broth. Continue to stir, heat to boiling, and boil and stir one minute. Immediately remove from heat. Serve over roast and vegetables.

Cajun rice with Hamburger and Vegetables

1 cup instant brown rice uncooked
½ pound lean hamburger
1 shallot, chopped fine
2 cups water
1 (14 oz) bag frozen pepper strips, or 2 bell peppers cut into strips (green peppers work best)
4 teaspoons Cajun seasoning recipe

Cook hamburger and shallot together until hamburger is browned. Drain. Set aside. Prepare the rice as directed on the package, except add Cajun seasoning to the water, and use 2 cups water. Add hamburger mixture to the rice once the water is boiling. Simmer until rice is tender. Combine all ingredients, including peppers, in a skillet and toss over medium-high heat for 4 to 5 minutes, or until peppers are at desired consistency and water has evaporated.

Chili

1 pound lean ground beef
2 shallots, chopped
4 cloves garlic, minced
1 cup water
1 ½ tablespoons chili powder
1 teaspoon salt
1 teaspoon ground cumin
1 teaspoon oregano
½ teaspoon ground cayenne pepper
1 can diced tomatoes
1 can kidney beans (check ingredients)

Brown beef, shallots, and garlic in a skillet. Drain. Put beef mixture and all remaining ingredients in large saucepan. Heat to boiling. Reduce heat and simmer for 30 minutes, stirring occasionally. Add water while cooking if necessary.

Enchiladas

1 tablespoon olive oil
1-2 shallots, chopped fine
2 cloves garlic, minced
3-4 cooked chicken breasts, cubed or shredded, or 1 taco filling recipe
¼ cup + ¾ cup "salsa with tomato and herbs" recipe
1 (4 oz) can chopped green chilies, drained (check ingredients)
4 oz cream cheese or Neufchatel cheese
1 teaspoon dried cilantro
7-8 flour or corn tortillas
3-4 slices high-quality American cheese, optional
½ cup chicken broth or water

Preheat oven to 375 degrees. Saute shallots and garlic in olive oil over medium heat for approximately 2 minutes, or until shallots are tender. Add ¼ cup of the salsa, the chilies, cream cheese, cilantro, and chicken. Add the chicken broth, then stir and heat thoroughly. You may stir in the American cheese at this time if you wish. Spray a 9 by 13 inch baking dish with non-stick cooking spray. Fill tortillas with chicken mixture and place side by side, seam side down in dish. Top with remaining salsa. Bake approximately 25 minutes or until thoroughly heated.

Fajitas

2 teaspoons chili powder
1 ½ teaspoons ground cumin
1 teaspoon garlic powder
¼ teaspoon cayenne pepper
1 boneless beef sirloin steak, fat trimmed from sides and beat to 1-1 ½ inches
      thick
2 shallots, cut into strips
2 bell peppers, cut into strips
2 cloves garlic, chopped
1 tomato, chopped
1 cup "soy" sauce recipe
7-8 flour tortillas

Preheat the broiler. Mix together chili powder, cumin, garlic powder, and cayenne pepper and rub over steak. Place on broiler pan rack and cook 6-10 minutes on each side, or to desired doneness. While steak is cooking, combine vegetables and sauce in a wok or saute pan and toss over medium heat until at desired consistency. Cut steak into strips and toss in vegetables for one minute. Remove from heat. Fill flour tortillas and enjoy.

Hamburgers

½ medium leek, chopped
1 pound lean hamburger meat
½ teaspoon garlic salt
¼ teaspoon pepper

Blend spices into hamburger meat with hands, then form into thin patties. Cook on a skillet or on the grill. Top with lettuce, tomatoes, and other preferred toppings and enjoy. Use condiments sparingly.

Hamburger Pie

1 pound lean ground beef
1 leek, chopped fine
½ teaspoon salt
½ teaspoon garlic powder
3 to 4 large cabbage leaves
5 High quality American cheese slices (from the deli counter)
2 large eggs
1 cup milk
½ cup all-purpose flour or wheat flour
½ tablespoon sugar
1 tablespoon canola or olive oil
2 teaspoons baking powder
1/8 teaspoon salt

Preheat oven to 400 degrees. Spray a 9-inch pie plate with non-stick spray and set aside. Brown beef, leek, ½ teaspoon salt, and garlic powder, and cook until beef is browned. Drain. Boil cabbage leaves for 4 to 5 minutes. Drain, pat dry, and tear into bite size pieces. Stir hamburger and cabbage together. Spread in pie plate and top with cheese in a single layer. Stir remaining ingredients together in a bowl. Batter may be slightly lumpy. Pour over cheese. Bake approximately 25 minutes or until top is slightly browned.
*This recipe was inspired by Bisquick's Cheeseburger Pie recipe.

Lasagna

1 package lasagna noodles, cooked and set in cold water for easier handling
1 recipe spaghetti sauce
1 15 oz. container ricotta cheese
1 egg

Mix cheese and egg in a bowl. Spray a thin layer of non-stick spray on lasagna pan. Lay a layer of lasagna noodles across the bottom of the pan. Then spread a layer of the cheese and egg mixture, followed by a layer of sauce. Repeat these steps one more time and top with another layer of noodles. Top with the remaining sauce. Bake covered in a 350 degree oven for 30-35 minutes, or until lasagna is no longer cold in the middle.

Taco and Burrito Filling

1 tablespoon olive oil
1 to 2 shallots, chopped fine
2 cloves garlic, minced
1 pound lean ground beef
2 ½ teaspoons chili powder
1/8 teaspoon ground cayenne pepper, optional
Salt and pepper to taste

Saute shallots in oil for 2 minutes in a large frying pan. Add garlic and saute 2 minutes more.   Add beef and remaining ingredients and cook until beef is browned. Drain. Make taco salad or burritos and top with *salsa with tomato and herb* recipe.

Meatloaf

1 ½ pounds extra lean ground beef or ground turkey
¾ cup milk
½ teaspoon sage
½ teaspoon salt
½ teaspoon dry ground mustard
¼ teaspoon pepper
½ teaspoon garlic powder
1 large egg
3 to 4 slices bread, torn into small pieces
2 shallots, chopped fine
¾ cup Barbecue Sauce recipe

Preheat oven to 350 degrees. Mix all ingredients together and spread in 9 by 5 inch loaf pan. Bake approximately one hour or until meat thermometer placed in center reaches 160 degrees. Let cool 10 minutes and remove from pan. Slice and serve.

Shepherd's Pie

½ pound lean hamburger
1 shallot, chopped fine
1 recipe cream of mushroom soup
½ cup tomato paste + ¼ cup water, optional, for tomato-based pie
1 packet Splenda sweetener or 2 teaspoons sugar, optional, for sweet tomato-based pie
1 (14 oz) can corn, drained
1 (14 oz) can green beans, drained
1 recipe mashed potatoes

Preheat oven to 375 degrees. Brown shallot and hamburger together. Drain and set aside. Combine soup, tomato paste + water, and Splenda. Add hamburger. Stir in corn and green beans and spread in a casserole dish. Top with mashed potatoes. Bake for 35 minutes, or until hot in center and bubbly around the edges.

Spaghetti Sauce

½ to 1 pound lean ground beef, optional
1 leek, finely chopped
2 cloves garlic, minced
1 (12 oz.) can tomato paste
1 (14 oz.) can diced tomatoes, blended in a food processor or blender if desired
1 ½ cups water
1 teaspoon dried basil
1 teaspoon dried oregano
1 teaspoon garlic powder
1/8 teaspoon ground thyme
1 packet Splenda sweetener or 2 teaspoons sugar, optional
Salt and pepper to taste

Cook hamburger together with leek and garlic until browned. Drain. Add tomato paste, diced tomatoes, and water. Stir in the remaining ingredients and simmer for approximately 25 minutes. Add more water to thin sauce if needed. Serve over spaghetti noodles.

Stuffed Green Peppers

4 medium green bell peppers, stems and seeds removed
1 pound cooked lean ground beef
1 recipe Spanish rice
6 ounces tomato paste
1 ½ cups water
½ teaspoon salt
½ teaspoon chili powder
½ teaspoon garlic powder

Preheat oven to 375 degrees. Boil peppers in enough water to cover for about 5 minutes. Add the ground beef to the Spanish rice. Stir remaining ingredients in small saucepan and heat thoroughly to make a sauce. Place peppers upright in square 8-inch baking dish and fill with rice and beef mixture. Pour tomato sauce mixture over peppers. Cover and bake for 30 minutes.

Swiss Steak

¼ cup olive oil
2 shallots, sliced
1 green pepper, chopped
¼ cup chopped celery
3-4 medium potatoes, cut into bite size pieces
1 ½ to 2 pounds beef round steak, cut about 2 inches thick
¼ cup all-purpose flour
1 (14 ounce) can diced tomatoes
1 cup water
1 teaspoon salt
½ teaspoon pepper

In heavy skillet, saute shallots, green pepper, and celery in olive oil over medium-high heat until tender. Pound flour into both sides of the steak and brown evenly in the pan. Add remaining ingredients. Reduce heat, cover and simmer for 1 to 1 ½ hours, or until meat and vegetables are tender. Add water as needed.

Chickpea Burgers

1 tablespoon olive oil
2 shallots, chopped
¾ cup mushrooms, chopped
3 cloves garlic, chopped
1 green pepper, chopped
1 15 oz can garbanzo beans, undrained
1 teaspoon garlic powder
1 teaspoon dried cilantro
½ teaspoon dried parsley
½ teaspoon ground cumin
1 cup dried bread crumbs
2 eggs
Olive oil
1 teaspoon salt
½ teaspoon pepper

Saute shallots, green pepper and mushrooms in a large skillet over medium heat until tender. Add garlic and saute a little bit more, but do not burn. Blend beans in a blender until smooth. Stir beans and mushroom mixture together in a large bowl. Stir in spices. Add bread crumbs and eggs and mix together until thoroughly blended. Heat olive oil in a large skillet, just enough to cover the bottom of the pan. Flatten bean mixture into thin patties and fry for approximately 5 minutes on each side, or until nicely browned. Salt and pepper as needed and drain on paper towels. Serve hot.

Barbecue Sauce, Cajun Seasoning, Ranch Dressing

Salad Dressings, Condiments and Sauces

Vinaigrette

½ cup olive oil
¼ cup distilled white vinegar
½ teaspoon salt
½ teaspoon pepper

Shake all ingredients until well blended in a covered container. Refrigerate and shake before serving.

Italian Salad Dressing

½ cup olive oil
½ cup white distilled vinegar
1 shallot, finely chopped
½ teaspoon salt
2 teaspoons sugar or 1 packet Splenda granular
1 teaspoon ground dry mustard
1 teaspoon basil
½ teaspoon oregano
½ teaspoon pepper
2 cloves garlic, crushed

Shake all ingredients until well blended in a covered container. Refrigerate and shake before serving. *For Creamy Italian, beat ¼ cup mayonnaise, heavy cream or half and half along with all other ingredients listed above in a large mixing bowl with electric mixer.

Tangy Ranch Dressing

1 cup mayonnaise
1/3 cup milk
2 tablespoons distilled white vinegar
½ teaspoon olive oil
1 teaspoon garlic powder
¼ teaspoon salt
1/8 teaspoon pepper
1/8 teaspoon paprika
½ teaspoon dried parsley
½ teaspoon dried dill weed

Place all ingredients in a blender. Cover and blend on medium speed until smooth, about 1 minute. Remove to container. Refrigerate leftovers.

Barbecue Sauce

½ teaspoon salt
Dash of paprika
½ teaspoon ground dry mustard
5 tablespoons light brown sugar, packed
½ teaspoon garlic powder
½ teaspoon pepper
1/8 teaspoon ground red (cayenne) pepper
1 tablespoon light corn syrup
3 tablespoons tomato paste
5 tablespoons butter or olive oil
2 tablespoons distilled white vinegar
3 to 4 tablespoons water

Stir all ingredients together in a saucepan and cook until boiling. Remove from heat. Top your favorite ribs or chicken and cook as directed.

Cajun Seasoning

2 teaspoons salt
2 teaspoons paprika
1 teaspoon ground cayenne pepper
2 teaspoons garlic powder
2 teaspoons ground thyme
1 teaspoon ground cumin, optional

Mix together, place in a seasoning shaker, and sprinkle over your favorite recipes.

Creamy Pan Sauce

1 tablespoon olive or canola oil
1 clove garlic, minced
2 tablespoons flour
1 cup chicken stock
4 oz cream cheese or Neufchatel cheese, cubed
½ teaspoon garlic salt

Saute garlic in oil over low heat for approximately 2 minutes. Add flour to form a paste. Slowly add chicken stock, stirring constantly, until smooth. Add cream cheese and garlic salt and stir until melted. Top your favorite noodles or main dish and enjoy!

Ketchup

1 tablespoon olive oil
½ shallot, minced
1 (6 oz.) can tomato paste
2 tablespoons white distilled vinegar
3 tablespoons brown sugar
1 ½ teaspoons garlic powder
1 teaspoon salt
1/8 teaspoon ginger
1/8 teaspoon cloves
¼ teaspoon cumin
1 tablespoon light corn syrup
1 cup water

Saute shallots in oil over medium heat for approximately 5 minutes, or until very tender. Add remaining ingredients and simmer for about one hour, or until mixture is at the correct consistency. Sauce will thicken a bit upon cooling.

Sunflower Seed Butter

½ pound sunflower seeds, de-shelled and de-skinned
Mild cooking oil (canola or grapeseed oil works well)
¼ teaspoon salt, more to taste if desired

Be sure to remove any bad seeds as this will spoil the batch. Blend sunflower seeds in a food processor or blender. Add a tiny amount of cooking oil when seeds are near correct consistency, just enough to make a smooth texture. Add salt and blend to desired consistency. Spread over toast or celery and enjoy!

"Soy" Sauce

1 cup beef stock (from preparing a beef roast in water)
2 teaspoons distilled white vinegar
1 teaspoon brown sugar
¼ teaspoon ground ginger
½ teaspoon garlic powder
¼ teaspoon pepper
1 teaspoon salt

Stir all ingredients together in a bowl and cook with your favorite foods. Or, heat in a pan to mix flavors and chill for future use.

"Teriyaki" Sauce

1 cup beef stock (from preparing a beef roast in water)
½ cup chicken stock
3 teaspoons distilled white vinegar
¾ cup packed brown sugar
¼ teaspoon ground ginger
½ teaspoon garlic powder
¼ teaspoon pepper
½ teaspoon salt

Stir all ingredients together in a saucepan over medium heat until boiling. Boil for one minute and remove from burner. Serve over your favorite recipe and enjoy.

Clam Chowder

Soups, Vegetables and Side Dishes

Clam Chowder

2 tablespoons butter or olive oil
2 shallots finely chopped
1 cup water
2 (6 ½ ounce) cans whole or minced clams, well drained
2 medium potatoes, chopped
1 teaspoon dried parsley
¼ teaspoon dried thyme
1 teaspoon salt
¼ teaspoon pepper
Chopped celery or carrots, if desired
2 cups milk

Saute shallots with butter in Dutch oven until tender. Add all remaining ingredients except milk. Bring to boiling, and boil until potatoes are tender. Add milk and heat thoroughly. Do not boil as this will spoil the milk.

Cream of Mushroom Soup

5 tablespoons butter or olive oil
1 cup mushrooms, chopped
1 shallot, chopped fine
2 cloves garlic, minced
¼ cup all-purpose flour
1 teaspoon salt
¼ teaspoon pepper
1 cup water
1 cup chicken stock (you may add water to it if you do not have enough)
1 cup milk

Saute mushrooms, shallot, and garlic in 2 tablespoons butter for 2 to 3 minutes. Add remaining butter, flour, salt, and pepper. Stir constantly over low heat until smooth and bubbly. Stir in water and chicken stock. Heat to boiling while stirring constantly. Add milk and heat thoroughly, but do not boil as this will spoil the milk.

Cream of Broccoli Soup
Omit mushrooms.   Add 1 large bag frozen broccoli or 1 ½ pounds chopped fresh broccoli along with the milk, and heat until broccoli is tender.

Cream of Chicken Soup
Omit mushrooms. Add ½ to 1 pound finely chopped or shredded cooked, seasoned chicken along with the milk.

Vegetable Beef Stew

1 lean beef roast weighing approximately 1 ½ pounds, or stew meat
1 shallot, chopped
1 cup water
Salt and pepper to taste
Water
6 medium carrots, peeled and cut
4 medium potatoes, peeled and cut
1 medium head cabbage, chopped
1 can diced tomatoes, optional
1 small bag frozen corn
1 small bag frozen green beans

Simmer roast, shallot, and 1 cup water for 1-1 ½ hours in Dutch oven. Cut roast into bite size pieces and place back into the pot. Add all remaining ingredients and boil for one hour.

Baked Beans

2 cans Great Northern beans, drained (check ingredients)
¾ cup packed brown sugar
1 teaspoon salt
½ teaspoon pepper
½ teaspoon dry ground mustard
2 shallots, chopped
2 teaspoons chili powder
water

Preheat oven to 350 degrees. Stir all ingredients except water together in a baking dish, and then add enough water to almost cover the beans. Bake uncovered for 30-45 minutes or until beans are hot and juice is bubbly around the edges.

Baked Potatoes

6 medium baking potatoes

Preheat oven to 375 degrees. Wash and lightly scrub potatoes to loosen dirt. Pierce potatoes with fork to allow steam to escape. Bake 1 to 1 ¼ hours.

For faster potatoes: bake 2 potatoes at a time in the microwave, on high, for 7 to 10 minutes. Note: Microwave ovens vary.

Coleslaw

1 medium head cabbage, shredded
2-3 carrots, shredded
1 cup milk
¼ cup sugar or Splenda granular
2 tablespoons distilled white vinegar

Combine all ingredients in a bowl and serve chilled.

Tasty Couscous

1 ½ cups chicken stock (you may add water if you do not have enough)
2 tablespoons butter
1 teaspoon green olive juice
¾ teaspoon salt
1 ½ cups plain couscous

Heat all ingredients except couscous in a saucepan and bring to a boil. Take pan off burner and add couscous. Stir and place lid back on the pan. Let stand as directed on package, or until couscous is at desired consistency. Fluff with fork and serve.

Creamy Noodles

7 ounces thin spaghetti, fettuccine, or egg noodles
3 teaspoons olive oil
1 shallot, chopped fine
1 clove garlic, chopped
½ cup cold water or chicken stock
3 teaspoons flour
2 ounces cream cheese
½ teaspoon paprika
½ teaspoon pepper
½ teaspoon salt
½ teaspoon garlic powder
¾ cup milk

Saute shallot and garlic in olive oil for approximately 2 minutes. Mix water and flour together in a cup until smooth. Add water mixture and cream cheese to pan, and stir until cream cheese is melted. Add milk and spices and heat thoroughly, but do not boil. Boil spaghetti noodles as directed on package, or add a little bit of chicken stock and salt to the water to add flavor. Pour sauce over spaghetti noodles and let sit for 3 minutes to allow sauce to thicken.

Fried Squash or Zucchini

1 or 2 yellow squash or zucchini
Olive oil
1/2 cup flour
¼ cup cornmeal
½ cup milk
1 egg
Salt and pepper to taste

Cut squash into straws and coat each piece with flour. Cover the bottom of a large frying pan with a thin coating of oil, and heat on medium-low setting. Blend milk and egg in one bowl, and flour and cornmeal in another bowl. Dip squash in milk mixture, then coat with flour mixture. Cook squash, making sure each piece fully touches the bottom of the pan. Turn and brown the other side. Dry on paper towel. Lightly dust with salt and pepper while still hot.

Garlic Broccoli and Cauliflower

2 tablespoons butter or olive oil
2 cloves garlic, minced
1 bag frozen cauliflower
1 bag frozen broccoli

Saute garlic cloves in the butter for 2 minutes, over medium heat, in a large skillet. Add broccoli and cauliflower and toss occasionally over medium-low heat until at desired consistency.

Glazed Carrots

1 bag frozen carrot slices
5 tablespoons butter or olive oil
¼ cup packed light brown sugar
Salt and pepper to taste

Cook carrots in boiling water approximately 10 minutes, or to desired tenderness. Lightly salt and pepper. Set aside. Melt butter in a heavy-bottomed pan and stir in brown sugar. When the butter and sugar are well blended, add the carrots and cook until well glazed.

Greek Style Green Beans

1/3 cup olive oil
1 shallot, chopped
2 cloves garlic, minced
1 package frozen green beans
1 16-ounce can diced tomatoes
2 teaspoons sugar or 1 packet Splenda sweetener
1 teaspoon garlic powder
1 teaspoon oregano
Salt and pepper to taste

Saute shallot and garlic in olive oil for approximately 3 minutes. Add all other ingredients and simmer, covered, for 30 to 45 minutes, or until green beans are soft and liquid is nearly evaporated.

Green Bean Casserole

1 recipe Cream of Mushroom Soup
4 (14 oz.) cans green beans, drained, or fresh or frozen green beans cooked
Potato chips, crushed, or Fried Onion Topping below

Preheat oven to 350 degrees. Mix soup and green beans together in a 9 by 13 rectangular baking dish. Bake for 20 minutes. Top with crushed potato chips or Fried onion topping. Bake 10 minutes more, or until edges are hot and bubbly.

Fried Onion Topping

Olive oil
6 shallots
1 cup white flour
1 cup cornmeal
1 teaspoon salt
½ teaspoon pepper

Slice shallots. Pull slices apart to make thin rings. Saute in oil for approximately two minutes to soften. Mix flour, cornmeal, salt, and pepper together. Fry with onions until lightly browned. Add more olive oil as needed.

Italian Potatoes

5 to 6 medium potatoes, cut into bite size pieces
2 shallots, coarsely chopped
1 teaspoons dried crushed rosemary
2 cloves garlic, finely chopped
½ teaspoon salt
½ teaspoon pepper
¼ cup olive oil

Preheat oven to 350 degrees. Stir all ingredients together in a 9 by 13 inch baking dish. Bake approximately one hour or until potatoes are tender.

Refried Beans

¼ cup olive oil
2 shallots, chopped
4 cloves garlic, crushed
1 cup water
1 can Pinto Beans, check ingredients
1 ½ teaspoons salt
½ teaspoon dried cumin

Heat oil in skillet. Saute shallots in oil for approximately 3 minutes, then add garlic and saute one more minute. Place beans and water in the pan and mash beans with a fork. Add remaining ingredients and more water until beans are at desired consistency. Top with salsa recipe, if desired, and enjoy!

Roasted Sweet Potatoes

Very good, but only for sweet potato lovers!

¼ cup olive oil
½ cup chicken stock
½ teaspoon oregano
½ teaspoon basil
½ teaspoon salt
2 teaspoons cinnamon
½ cup brown sugar
2 cloves garlic, minced
3 large sweet potatoes, cut into cubes
2 shallots, sliced

Preheat oven to 425 degrees. Mix all ingredients together in a 9 by 13 inch baking dish. Bake for approximately 35 minutes, or until potatoes are tender.

Rosemary Squash

2 medium yellow squash
2 medium zucchini
Olive Oil
Dried crushed rosemary
Salt and pepper to taste

Preheat oven to 375 degrees. Cut squash and zucchini into large bite size pieces. Spread out evenly in a 9 by 13 inch baking dish. Drizzle lightly with olive oil. Sprinkle lightly with rosemary, salt, and pepper. Toss to coat evenly. Bake 20-30 minutes or to desired tenderness.

Spanish Rice

2 tablespoons olive oil
1 shallot, chopped
1 cup uncooked instant brown rice
2 ¼ cups water
1 ½ teaspoons salt
1 teaspoon chili powder
½ teaspoon garlic powder
6 ounces tomato paste

Heat oil in large skillet over medium heat. Saute shallot in oil for 3-5 minutes, or until tender. Add remaining ingredients and stir until rice is at desired consistency (about 10 minutes).

Squash Apple Bake

2 pounds yellow squash
2 baking apples
½ cup packed brown sugar
¼ cup butter
1 tablespoon flour
1 teaspoon salt

Preheat oven to 350 degrees. Peel the squash, then cut into cubes. Prepare the apples the same way, but remove the core and seeds. Stir together remaining ingredients and set aside. Arrange squash in ungreased 9 by 13 inch baking dish. Top with apple slices. Sprinkle sugar mixture over the top. Cover and bake for 50 to 60 minutes or until squash and apples are tender. (Thanks for the recipe Grandma)

Summer Tomatoes

5 or 6 fresh tomatoes
4 shallots, chopped
¼ cup olive oil
¼ cup white distilled vinegar
1 teaspoon dried basil
1 loaf French bread (at least one day old with no trigger preservatives), optional

Slice tomatoes and place on a serving dish. Mix shallots, oil and vinegar together and pour over the tomatoes. Sprinkle basil on top. Refrigerate for a few hours to let flavors set in. Enjoy the tomatoes and dip bread in the marinade, if desired.

Twice Baked Sweet Potatoes

4 large sweet potatoes
4 oz cream cheese or Neufchatel cheese, softened
4 tablespoons butter, softened
¼ cup milk
¼ cup packed brown sugar
2 tablespoons ground cinnamon

Preheat oven to 375 degrees. Bake potatoes one hour to one hour and 15 minutes. Remove from oven and let cool until able to handle. Cut potatoes lengthwise in half and scoop out centers into a medium size mixing bowl. Add remaining ingredients and blend. Spoon mixture back into potato shells and bake approximately 20 minutes or until thoroughly heated.

Final Thoughts

The layout or format for this cookbook was inspired by those of traditional cookbooks and many others that I've had the pleasure of reading. I wanted to make it as easy as possible for you to get around in your kitchen. Some recipes were inspired by those given to me by family members and friends, and I appreciate their donations. All recipes were created through careful thought and consideration of the types of foods migraine sufferers, including myself, might be looking for. I hope you enjoy them.

Sincerely,
Heidi Gunderson

For updates, blogs, migraine support, and new recipes:

- **www.migrainefreecooking.com**
- **www.migrainefreecooking.blogspot.com**
- **www.twitter.com/migrainecooking**

References

There are many wonderful resources for migraines. I'm sure you have encountered some on your migraine-free journey. I included some websites that might be helpful if you are interested. Still, it is necessary to read *Heal Your Headache* by Dr. Buchholz to truly understand your migraines.

"American Headache Society" 2009 <http://www.americanheadachesociety.org>.
The American Headache Society is one of the leading organizations for headache advocacy and research.

Buchholz, David, M.D. <u>Heal Your Headache: The 1-2-3 Program for Taking Charge of Your Pain</u> New York, NY: Workman Publishing. 2002.
It is essential that you read this book as well as mine.

"National Headache Foundation" 2009 <http://www.headaches.org>.
The National Headache Foundation is one of the leading organizations for headache advocacy and research.

Index